At Issue

Transgender People

Other Books in the At Issue Series:

At Issue

Transgender People

Tamara Thompson, Book Editor

GREENHAVEN PRESS
A part of Gale, Cengage Learning

GALE
CENGAGE Learning·

Farmington Hills, Mich • San Francisco • New York • Waterville, Maine
Meriden, Conn • Mason, Ohio • Chicago

GALE
CENGAGE Learning

Patricia Coryell, *Vice President & Publisher, New Products & GVRL*
Douglas Dentino, *Manager, New Products*
Judy Galens, *Acquisitions Editor*

For more information, contact:
Greenhaven Press
27500 Drake Rd.
Farmington Hills, MI 48331-3535
Or you can visit our Internet site at gale.cengage.com

For product information and technology assistance, contact us at

Gale Customer Support, 1-800-877-4253
For permission to use material from this text or product, submit all requests online at www.cengage.com/permissions.

Further permissions questions can be e-mailed to permissionrequest@cengage.com.

Articles in Greenhaven Press anthologies are often edited for length to meet page require-ments. In addition, original titles of these works are changed to clearly present the main thesis and to explicitly indicate the author's opinion. Every effort is made to ensure that Greenhaven Press accurately reflects the original intent of the authors. Every effort has been made to trace the owners of copyrighted material.

Cover photograph copyright © Images.com/Corbis.

LIBRARY OF CONGRESS CATALOGING-IN-PUBLICATION DATA

Transgender people / Tamara Thompson, book editor.
    pages cm. -- (At issue)
    Includes bibliographical references and index.
    ISBN 978-0-7377-7191-6 (hardback) -- ISBN 978-0-7377-7192-3 (paperback)
    1. Transgender people--Juvenile literature. 2. Gender identity--Juvenile litera-ture. I. Thompson, Tamara.
    HQ77.9.T71592 2015
    306.76'8--dc23
                                                                    2014034672

Printed in Mexico
1 2 3 4 5 6 7 19 18 17 16 15

Contents

Introduction

Long relegated to the margins of both mainstream society and the LGBT (lesbian, gay, bisexual, and transgender) movement, the transgender community is finally having a coming-out party of its own, and making quantum leaps both culturally and politically.

Although transgender people are benefitting from recent landmark legal gains and a meteoric rise in pop culture, the 1.5 million Americans who identify as transgender continue to face deeply entrenched systemic discrimination, widespread misunderstanding, and powerful political backlash.

According to the National Center for Transgender Equality (NCTE), "numerous studies have shown that transgender people face disproportionate amounts of discrimination in all areas of life," and that persistent patterns of abuse mean trans people are more likely to live in extreme poverty, experience harassment, bullying, and sexual assault, and be denied housing, jobs, and health care simply because of their trans status. A shocking 41 percent of transgender people have attempted suicide, compared to just 1.6 percent of the general population, according to the NCTE.

The term "transgender" or "trans" doesn't just refer to people who have had or want a sex-change operation to make their bodies match their internal feelings of who they are; it applies to many different kinds of people who don't fit neatly into society's binary concept of gender being strictly male/female.

Experts say that sex, gender, and sexual orientation are distinctly different things that, while aligned in a predictable way for most people, don't actually depend on each other. *Sex* is biological; it describes the sex chromosomes, hormones, reproductive organs, and genitals that a person has. *Gender*, though, is a cultural construct; its meaning is learned from experiences, and that learning leads to one's internal sense of *gender identity*, of feeling male or female—or perhaps neither or both. *Sexual orientation*, meanwhile, simply describes what kind of sexual partner a person is attracted to.

While most people's internal gender identity and biological sex match (known as being cisgender), for transgender people that is not the case and it can cause an overwhelming sense of distress and incongruity.

Although many trans people are content to express their nonconforming gender identities through clothing, hairstyle, mannerisms, and other ways of presenting themselves, others seek to radically transform their bodies—through hormone therapy and surgery—to match their gender identities, a process commonly known as "transitioning."

There is broad medical consensus that "gender affirming" treatments to facilitate such a transition are medically necessary for transgender people who desire it. A trans man is a biological female who has transitioned to male; a trans woman is a biological male who has transitioned to female. Like cisgender people, transgender people may identify as gay, straight, or bisexual in their sexual orientation.

For several decades, transgenderism was considered a mental disorder known as "gender identity disorder," but in December 2012, the American Psychiatric Association (APA) changed its diagnostic criteria so that simply "being trans" is no longer considered a mental illness but rather a normal human gender variant. A newly created diagnosis of "gender dysphoria" is now only invoked if a person's transgender status causes them significant stress or disability.

Although 65 percent of Americans know someone who is gay or lesbian, less than 10 percent know a transgender person. But that unfamiliarity is beginning to fade as trans people become more visible in mainstream culture and individuals increasingly come out as trans to their families, friends, and coworkers.

Transgender celebrities such as trans man Chaz Bono on *Dancing with the Stars*, and Laverne Cox, a trans woman playing a trans character on the popular Netflix series *Orange Is the New Black*, have brought transgender awareness into the American living room for the first time, and ignited a blaze of public interest in the process.

Major fashion labels now feature trans models in their ads and trans contestants are fan favorites on reality television shows such as *Project Runway*. A transgender memoir by former *People* magazine editor Janet Mock recently made the *New York Times* bestseller list, while Mock herself cheerfully made the rounds on the television talk show circuit.

But behind the public's recent fascination with transgender people in the entertainment world, there is also some serious substance.

"When people have points of reference that are humanizing, that demystifies difference," Mock told *TIME*, magazine as part of its groundbreaking June 2014 cover story, "The Transgender Tipping Point," which media critics have called "the most positive and in-depth representation of transgender life experiences ever presented in mainstream print media."

Indeed, the political momentum of the transgender movement is as unmistakable as its cultural momentum.

Long viewed as an ally of the LGBT community, Barack Obama is the first president to ever use the word "transgender" in a speech, and Vice President Joe Biden has called transgender rights "the civil rights issue of our time."

During Obama's first term, he signed hate-crime legislation that included the nation's first federal civil rights protections for transgender people. "Since then," writes the Associated Press, "the administration has quietly applied the power of the executive branch to make it easier for transgender people to update their passports, obtain health insurance under the Affordable Care Act, get treatment at Veteran's Administration facilities and seek access to public school restrooms and sports programs—just a few of the transgender-specific policy shifts of Obama's presidency."

The others have been no less significant. In 2014 alone:

- The US Department of Health and Human Services scrapped a longstanding rule that prohibited the government's Medicare health insurance program for seniors from covering sex-reassignment surgeries. Two weeks later, the government agreed to do the same for federal employees.

- The president signed an executive order prohibiting the federal government and businesses that hold federal contracts from discriminating on the basis of sexual orientation or transgender status, the first workplace protection of its kind.

- A government commission concluded that there is no medical reason to prohibit transgender people from serving in the military and recommended that the current ban be lifted.

- The US Department of Education affirmed that transgender students are entitled to federal civil rights protections under Title IX, the law that bans gender discrimination in education.

- California became the first state to enact a statute allowing transgender students to choose the bathroom facilities and sports teams of their preferred gender. (Massachusetts and Connecticut have similar policies but not actual statutes.)

While transgender people and their advocates celebrate these public policy milestones, however, those who oppose transgender rights amid the gender identity movement have shifted into high gear to fight what they see as a dangerous threat to traditional family values and inviolable cultural norms.

"The tiny minority of individuals who self-identify as 'transgender' are asking the rest of society to not only affirm them in their gender confusion and pain, but to radically re-order the ways in which the culture makes reasonable and rational accommodation for the two genders," the influential conservative Christian group Focus on the Family warns on its website. "If the transgender lobby succeeds, there will be striking consequences for marriage, family and society at large. . . . This is a cultural and theological battle that we must engage and win."

The authors included in *At Issue: Transgender People* represent a wide range of viewpoints about what it means to be transgender, how far the government and social institutions should go to accommodate transgender people, and the role of health care in the lives of transgender children and adults.

What Does It Mean to Be Transgender?

American Psychological Association

The American Psychological Association is the world's largest professional association of psychologists.

There are many nuances to the concepts of gender, gender identity, sex, and sexual orientation. Transgender is a term that describes many different types of people whose expression of gender falls outside traditional norms, including genderqueers, cross-dressers, drag queens and kings, and transsexuals—those whose gender identity is different from their biological sex. Many transsexuals choose to "transition" to the gender they identify with by altering their physical appearance to match their internal sense of being, often via hormone treatment or surgery. Transgenderism itself is no longer considered a mental disorder, but it can become one if it causes significant stress or disability to the individual.

*T*ransgender is an umbrella term for persons whose *gender identity*, *gender expression*, or behavior does not conform to that typically associated with the sex to which they were assigned at birth. *Gender identity* refers to a person's internal sense of being male, female, or something else; *gender expression* refers to the way a person communicates gender identity to others through behavior, clothing, hairstyles, voice, or body characteristics. "Trans" is sometimes used as shorthand for "transgender." While transgender is generally a good term to use, not everyone whose appearance or behavior is gender-nonconforming will identify as a transgender person. The ways that transgender people are talked about in popular culture, academia, and science are constantly changing, particularly as individuals' awareness, knowledge, and openness about transgender people and their experiences grow.

Sex is assigned at birth, refers to one's biological status as either male or female, and is associated primarily with physical attributes such as chromosomes, hormone prevalence, and external and internal anatomy. *Gender* refers to the socially constructed roles, behaviors, activities, and attributes that a given society considers appropriate for boys and men, or girls and women. These influence the ways that people act, interact, and feel about themselves. While aspects of biological sex are similar across different cultures, aspects of gender may differ.

Various conditions that lead to atypical development of physical sex characteristics are collectively referred to as *intersex conditions*. For information about people with intersex conditions (also known as disorders of sex development), see [The American Psychological Association] APA's brochure *Answers to Your Questions About Individuals With Intersex Conditions*.

Transgender persons have been documented in many indigenous, Western, and Eastern cultures and societies from antiquity until the present day. However, the meaning of gender nonconformity may vary from culture to culture.

What Are Some Types of Transgender People?

Many identities fall under the transgender umbrella. The term *transsexual* refers to people whose gender identity is different

13

from their assigned sex. Often, transsexual people alter or wish to alter their bodies through hormones, surgery, and other means to make their bodies as congruent as possible with their gender identities. This process of transition through medical intervention is often referred to as sex or gender reassignment, but more recently is also referred to as gender affirmation. People who were assigned female, but identify and live as male and alter or wish to alter their bodies through medical intervention to more closely resemble their gender identity are known as transsexual men or transmen (also known as female-to-male or FTM). Conversely, people who were assigned male, but identify and live as female and alter or wish to alter their bodies through medical intervention to more closely resemble their gender identity are known as transsexual women or transwomen (also known as male-to-female or MTF). Some individuals who transition from one gender to another prefer to be referred to as a man or a woman, rather than as transgender.

Experts believe that biological factors such as genetic influences and prenatal hormone levels, early experiences, and experiences later in adolescence or adulthood may all contribute to the development of transgender identities.

People who *cross-dress* wear clothing that is traditionally or stereotypically worn by another gender in their culture. They vary in how completely they cross-dress, from one article of clothing to fully cross-dressing. Those who cross-dress are usually comfortable with their assigned sex and do not wish to change it. Cross-dressing is a form of gender expression and is not necessarily tied to erotic activity. Cross-dressing is not indicative of sexual orientation. The degree of societal acceptance for cross-dressing varies for males and females. In some cultures, one gender may be given more latitude than another for wearing clothing associated with a different gender.

The term *drag queens* generally refers to men who dress as women for the purpose of entertaining others at bars, clubs, or other events. The term *drag kings* refers to women who dress as men for the purpose of entertaining others at bars, clubs, or other events.

Genderqueer is a term that some people use who identify their gender as falling outside the binary constructs of "male" and "female." They may define their gender as falling somewhere on a continuum between male and female, or they may define it as wholly different from these terms. They may also request that pronouns be used to refer to them that are neither masculine nor feminine, such as "zie" instead of "he" or "she," or "hir" instead of "his" or "her." Some genderqueer people do not identify as transgender.

Other categories of transgender people include androgynous, multigendered, gender nonconforming, third gender, and two-spirit people. Exact definitions of these terms vary from person to person and may change over time, but often include a sense of blending or alternating genders. Some people who use these terms to describe themselves see traditional, binary concepts of gender as restrictive.

Why Are Some People Transgender?

There is no single explanation for why some people are transgender. The diversity of transgender expression and experiences argues against any simple or unitary explanation. Many experts believe that biological factors such as genetic influences and prenatal hormone levels, early experiences, and experiences later in adolescence or adulthood may all contribute to the development of transgender identities.

It is difficult to accurately estimate the number of transgender people, mostly because there are no population studies that accurately and completely account for the range of gender identity and gender expression.

Gender identity and *sexual orientation* are not the same. *Sexual orientation* refers to an individual's enduring physical, romantic, and/or emotional attraction to another person, whereas *gender identity* refers to one's internal sense of being male, female, or something else. Transgender people may be straight, lesbian, gay, bisexual, or asexual, just as nontransgender people can be. Some recent research has shown that a change or a new exploration period in partner attraction may occur during the process of transition. However, transgender people usually remain as attached to loved ones after transition as they were before transition. Transgender people usually label their sexual orientation using their gender as a reference. For example, a transgender woman, or a person who is assigned male at birth and transitions to female, who is attracted to other women would be identified as a lesbian or gay woman. Likewise, a transgender man, or a person who is assigned female at birth and transitions to male, who is attracted to other men would be identified as a gay man.

How Does Someone Know They Are Transgender?

Transgender people experience their transgender identity in a variety of ways and may become aware of their transgender identity at any age. Some can trace their transgender identities and feelings back to their earliest memories. They may have vague feelings of "not fitting in" with people of their assigned sex or specific wishes to be something other than their assigned sex. Others become aware of their transgender identities or begin to explore and experience gender-nonconforming attitudes and behaviors during adolescence or much later in life. Some embrace their transgender feelings, while others struggle with feelings of shame or confusion. Those who transition later in life may have struggled to fit in adequately as their assigned sex only to later face dissatisfaction with their lives. Some transgender people, transsexuals in particular, experience intense dissatisfaction with their sex assigned at birth, physical sex characteristics, or the gender role associated with that sex. These individuals often seek gender-affirming treatments.

Parents may be concerned about a child who appears to be gender-nonconforming for a variety of reasons. Some children express a great deal of distress about their assigned sex at birth or the gender roles they are expected to follow. Some children experience difficult social interactions with peers and adults because of their gender expression. Parents may become concerned when what they believed to be a "phase" does not pass. Parents of gender-nonconforming children may need to work with schools and other institutions to address their children's particular needs and ensure their children's safety. It is helpful to consult with mental health and medical professionals familiar with gender issues in children to decide how to best address these concerns. It is not helpful to force the child to act in a more gender-conforming way. Peer support from other parents of gender-nonconforming children may also be helpful.

How Do Transsexuals Make a Gender Transition?

Transitioning from one gender to another is a complex process and may involve transition to a gender that is neither traditionally male nor female. People who transition often start by expressing their preferred gender in situations where they feel safe. They typically work up to living full time as members of their preferred gender by making many changes a little at a time. While there is no "right" way to transition genders, there are some common social changes transgender people experience that may involve one or more of the following: adopting the appearance of the desired sex through changes in clothing and grooming, adopting a new name, changing sex designation on identity documents (if possible), using hormone therapy treatment, and/or undergoing medical procedures that modify their body to conform with their gender identity.

Many transgender people do not experience their gender as distressing or disabling, which implies that identifying as transgender does not constitute a mental disorder.

Every transgender person's process or transition differs. Because of this, many factors may determine how the individual wishes to live and express their gender identity. Finding a qualified mental health professional who is experienced in providing affirmative care for transgender people is an important first step. A qualified professional can provide guidance and referrals to other helping professionals. Connecting with other transgender people through peer support groups and transgender community organizations is also helpful.

The World Professional Association for Transgender Health (WPATH), a professional organization devoted to the treatment of transgender people, publishes *The Standards of Care for Gender Identity Disorders,* which offers recommendations for the provision of gender affirmation procedures and services.

A psychological state is considered a mental disorder only if it causes significant distress or disability. Many transgender people do not experience their gender as distressing or disabling, which implies that identifying as transgender does not constitute a mental disorder. For these individuals, the significant problem is finding affordable resources, such as counseling, hormone therapy, medical procedures, and the social support necessary to freely express their gender identity and minimize discrimination. Many other obstacles may lead to distress, including a lack of acceptance within society, direct or indirect experiences with discrimination, or assault. These experiences may lead many transgender people to suffer with anxiety, depression, or related disorders at higher rates than nontransgender persons. . . .

What Kinds of Discrimination Do Transgender People Face?

Anti-discrimination laws in most U.S. cities and states do not protect transgender people from discrimination based on gender identity or gender expression. Consequently, transgender people in most cities and states face discrimination in nearly every aspect of their lives. The National Center for Transgender Equality and the National Gay and Lesbian Task Force released a report in 2011 entitled *Injustice at Every Turn*, which confirmed the pervasive and severe discrimination faced by transgender people. Out of a sample of nearly 6,500 transgender people, the report found that transgender people experience high levels of discrimination in employment, housing, health care, education, legal systems, and even in their families. The report can be found at http://endtransdiscrimination.org.

Transgender people may also have additional identities that may affect the types of discrimination they experience. Groups with such additional identities include transgender people of racial, ethnic, or religious minority backgrounds; transgender people of lower socioeconomic statuses; transgender people with disabilities; transgender youth; transgender elderly; and others. Experiencing discrimination may cause significant amounts of psychological stress, often leaving transgender individuals to wonder whether they were discriminated against because of their gender identity or gender expression, another sociocultural identity, or some combination of all of these.

According to the study, while discrimination is pervasive for the majority of transgender people, the intersection of anti-transgender bias and persistent, structural racism is especially severe. People of color in general fare worse than White transgender people, with African American transgender individuals faring far worse than all other transgender populations examined.

Many transgender people are the targets of hate crimes. They are also the victims of subtle discrimination—which includes everything from glances or glares of disapproval or discomfort to invasive questions about their body parts.

How Can I Be Supportive of Transgender People?

- Educate yourself about transgender issues by reading books, attending conferences, and consulting with transgender experts.

- Be aware of your attitudes concerning people with gender-nonconforming appearance or behavior.

- Know that transgender people have membership in various sociocultural identity groups (e.g., race, social class, religion, age, disability, etc.) and there is not one universal way to look or be transgender.

- Use names and pronouns that are appropriate to the person's gender presentation and identity; if in doubt, ask.

- Don't make assumptions about transgender people's sexual orientation, desire for hormonal or medical treatment, or other aspects of their identity or transition plans. If you have a reason to know (e.g., you are a physician conducting a necessary physical exam or you are a person who is interested in dating someone that you've learned is transgender), ask.

- Don't confuse gender nonconformity with being transgender. Not all people who appear androgynous or gender nonconforming identify as transgender or desire gender affirmation treatment.

- Keep the lines of communication open with the transgender person in your life.

- Get support in processing your own reactions. It can take some time to adjust to seeing someone you know well transitioning. Having someone close to you transition will be an adjustment and can be challenging, especially for partners, parents, and children.

- Seek support in dealing with your feelings. You are not alone. Mental health professionals and support groups for family, friends, and significant others of transgender people can be useful resources.

- Advocate for transgender rights, including social and economic justice and appropriate psychological care.

- Familiarize yourself with the local and state or provincial laws that protect transgender people from discrimination.

Being Transgender Is Not a Mental Disorder

Dana Beyer

Dana Beyer is the executive director of Gender Rights Maryland, a state-level organization dedicated to the protection of civil rights for transgender people.

In a major step forward for transgender rights and cultural acceptance, in 2012, the American Psychiatric Association (APA) changed the criteria used to diagnose mental disorders so that simply "being trans" is no longer considered a mental illness but rather a normal human gender variant. Transgender advocates say the change is as important as the APA's declassification of homosexuality as a disorder in 1973, and that the landmark change—along with other key moments of progress in both the courts and culture—signals the emergence of trans people from the margins of society.

The march forward for trans civil rights proceeds apace, its momentum unflagging. It was one year ago [December 2011] this week that Judge William Pryor of Alabama, a man not known for his sympathies for the LGBT [lesbian, gay, bisexual, and transgender] community, stated in the 11th Circuit Federal Court of Appeals in Atlanta [Georgia] that trans persons were a protected class under the 14th Amendment. Now the Board of Trustees of the American Psychiatric Association (APA) has ratified the [*Diagnostic and Statistical*

Manual of Mental Disorders–volume] DSM-5, the fifth edition of what is known colloquially as the "psychiatrists' bible," so as of Dec. 1, [2012] trans persons are no longer classified by the medical community as mentally ill, this decision coming 39 years after homosexuality was declassified as a mental illness by the same organization.

I have personally been involved in many civil rights campaigns, but as a physician, none has mattered more to me than this one. The fact that my medical colleagues now better understand basic human sexual biology is a source of both relief and pride. I can recall prowling the psychiatric literature in the stacks of the Uris and Olin libraries at Cornell [University] and the medical library at Penn [University of Pennsylvania], finding only the most egregiously vile descriptions of who I was as a human being. I recall making surgical rounds at Pennsylvania Hospital in 1976 and listening to the disparaging remarks made by attending physicians and students alike about a trans woman who had just undergone genital reconstruction. I recall the hate speech of opponents to trans anti-discrimination bills in the halls of Congress, Annapolis and Rockville, Md., constantly harping on the supposed mental illness of the gender-nonconforming and the threat we posed by our very existence.

There are many activists who feel that the APA didn't go far enough and oppose the mention of any form of cross-gender behavior.

A Major Step Forward

Don't underestimate the significance of this evolution. That we no longer have to take such talk seriously in the legislatures and courts and can roll our eyes as we do when fundamentalists chatter on about gay men showering with straight ones is a hugely positive change. That we now have the gender identity consultation staff at the Johns Hopkins School of

Medicine speaking out forcefully for comprehensive civil rights protections when not long ago we lived with the reality that Hopkins, with the infamous Emeritus Professor Paul McHugh as its spokesperson, was in the vanguard of denying trans women their humanity is remarkable progress. This is part of the cultural change that influences courts and legislatures, which, in turn, dialectically influence the culture. As an example, it would not be a reach to believe that the leadership of the corporate community on LGBT equality in Atlanta had a salient impact on Judge Pryor. Nor would it be hard to imagine that the quiet, dignified work of physicians Greg Lehne, Bill Reiner, Chris Kraft and others at Hopkins influenced the antediluvian opinions of Paul McHugh and his colleagues.

When the closing bell is rung, we should remember those who toiled through the decades with little expectation of recognition or success. Just as President [Barack] Obama's support of the trans and gay communities these past four years was only the final push of sufficiency needed to create so much change, this landmark achievement would not have been made possible without the yeomanly work of so many.

Individuals Worthy of Note

A few whom I feel are particularly noteworthy of mention are Jack Drescher, M.D., who has long been active on LGBT concerns within the APA; Edgardo Menvielle, M.D., who led the workgroup of the Washington Psychiatric Society, which rewrote the gender dysphoria text, and on which I was honored to serve; and Roger Peele, M.D., Chief Psychiatrist for Montgomery County, Md., a strong advocate for the trans community on the Board of Trustees of the APA. We all owe a great deal to Kelley Winters, Ph.D., who has been the conscience as well as the motivating force in the campaign to depathologize the state of being transgender.

I don't want to leave the impression that the job is complete. Just as the removal of homosexuality in 1973 was partial, the exclusion not completed until 1987, there is still work to be done for the broader trans community. The DSM still dehumanizes garden-variety cross-dressing under the category "transvestic fetishism," particularly insulting in its use of the term "fetish." And there are many activists who feel that the APA didn't go far enough and oppose the mention of any form of cross-gender behavior in the DSM, including the new category, "gender dysphoria."

From Mental Illness to Normal Variant

Still, while for many people the devil will be in the details, in its larger sociopolitical impact this ranks with the major de-classification of homosexuality in 1973. Our greatest accom-plishment on the Working Group was reconceptualizing the state of "being trans" from a mental illness to a normal hu-man variant. Now accepted by the American psychiatric com-munity (and years ago by the psychological), this conceptual-ization defangs the most potent arguments of the opposition, which often portrays trans women as sexual predators. Back in 1990 trans persons were lumped together with pedophiles in the Americans With Disabilities Act (ADA), reflective of a common misperception that trans women were inherently de-ceptive and fraudulent, monstrous beings whose only purpose was sexual assault on the innocent. This new edition of what passes for the consensus of the medical community regarding issues of sexuality finally brings trans persons into the light with the rest of the community of humanity.

3

There Is No Such Thing as "Transgender"

Thaddeus Baklinski

Thaddeus Baklinski is a staff writer for LifeSiteNews, a news website operated by the Campaign Life Coalition, a conservative Christian group.

From a medical and scientific standpoint, there is no such thing as a transgender person; all humans are either biologically male or female. Individuals who maintain they are trapped in bodies of the wrong gender are suffering from delusions and their distress is purely psychological. The appropriate treatment for such a case is mental health care, not sex-change surgery that reinforces a mental disorder rather than treating it. Many individuals who do have such surgery discover it does not solve their gender confusion problems. There is no reason to grant special rights to people who call themselves transgender, and laws that include protections for "gender identity" and "gender expression" are dangerous to society.

A prominent Toronto [Canada] psychiatrist has severely criticized the assumptions underlying what has been dubbed by critics as the Canadian federal government's "bathroom bill," that is, Bill C-279, a private member's bill that would afford special protection to so-called "transgender" men and women.

Dr. Joseph Berger has issued a statement saying that from a medical and scientific perspective there is no such thing as a "transgendered" person, and that terms such as "gender expression" and "gender identity" used in the bill are at the very least ambiguous, and are more an emotional appeal than a statement of scientific fact.

Berger, who is a consulting psychiatrist in Toronto and whose list of credentials establishes him as an expert in the field of mental illness, stated that people who identify themselves as "transgendered" are mentally ill or simply unhappy, and pointed out that hormone therapy and surgery are not appropriate treatments for psychosis or unhappiness.

"From a scientific perspective, let me clarify what 'transgendered' actually means," Dr. Berger said, adding, "I am speaking now about the scientific perspective—and not any political lobbying position that may be proposed by any group, medical or non-medical."

"'Transgendered' are people who claim that they really are or wish to be people of the sex opposite to which they were born, or to which their chromosomal configuration attests," Dr. Berger stated.

"Sometimes, some of these people have claimed that they are 'a woman trapped in a man's body' or alternatively 'a man trapped in a woman's body.'"

Surgery Is Not the Answer

"The medical treatment of delusions, psychosis or emotional happiness is not surgery," Dr. Berger stated.

"On the other hand," Dr. Berger continued, "if these people are asked to clarify exactly what they believe, that is to say do they truly believe whichever of those above propositions applies to them and they say 'no', then they know that such a proposition is not true, but that they 'feel' it, then what we are talking about scientifically, is just unhappiness, and that unhappiness is being accompanied by a wish—that leads some people into taking hormones that predominate in the other sex, and even having cosmetic surgery designed to make them 'appear' as if they are a person of the opposite sex."

There seems to me to be no medical or scientific reason to grant any special rights or considerations to people who are unhappy with the sex they were born into, or to people who wish to dress in the clothes of the opposite sex.

He explained that cosmetic surgery will not change the chromosomes of a human being in that it will not make a man become a woman, capable of menstruating, ovulating, and having children, nor will it make a woman into a man, capable of generating sperm that can unite with an egg or ovum from a woman and fertilize that egg to produce a human child.

Moreover, Dr. Berger stated that the arguments put forward by those advocating for special rights for gender confused people have no scientific value and are subjective and emotional appeals with no objective scientific basis.

"I have read the brief put forward by those advocating special rights, and I find nothing of scientific value in it," Dr. Berger said in his statement. "Words and phrases, such as 'the inner space,' are used that have no objective scientific basis."

"These are the scientific facts," Dr. Berger said. "There seems to me to be no medical or scientific reason to grant any special rights or considerations to people who are unhappy with the sex they were born into, or to people who wish to dress in the clothes of the opposite sex."

Gender Confusion Is Purely Psychological

"The so-called 'confusion' about their sexuality that a teenager or adult has is purely psychological. As a psychiatrist, I see no reason for people who identify themselves in these ways to have any rights or privileges different from everyone else in Canada," he concluded.

REAL [Realistic, Equal, Active, for Life] Women of Canada asked Dr. Berger for a statement on the issues surrounding Bill C-279 after the organization appeared before the review committee hearings on the bill.

Gwen Landolt of REAL Women told LifeSiteNews that after being initially refused permission to present their perspective on the bill to the review committee, the group was accepted, but found that all other groups and individuals who had been accepted to appear before the committee were supporters of Bill C-279.

"It can scarcely be an impartial review of any bill if only the witnesses supporting the bill are invited to speak to it," Landolt said.

Landolt explained that after passing second reading on June 6, 2012, Bill C-279 went to the Justice and Human Rights Committee for review.

At the review committee hearings, REAL Women of Canada presented a 12 page brief setting out the harms created by the bill, and pointing out that the terms "gender expression" and "gender identity," as written in Bill C-279, were so broad that they could be used to protect pedophilia along with other sexual perversions, if passed into law.

REAL Women provided the committee with evidence that post-operative trans-gendered individuals suffer substantially higher morbidity and mortality than the general population, placing the so-called "sex reassignment" surgery and hormone treatment under continued scrutiny.

Surgery Outcomes Prompt Reversal

They pointed out that a pioneer in such treatment, Dr. Paul McHugh, distinguished professor of psychiatry at Johns Hopkins University School of Medicine and psychiatrist-in-chief at

Johns Hopkins Hospital, stopped the procedures because he found that patients were no better adjusted or satisfied after receiving such treatment.

McHugh wrote in 2004 that "Hopkins was fundamentally cooperating with a mental illness" by catering to the desires of people who wanted surgery to change their biological sex.

"We psychiatrists, I thought, would do better to concentrate on trying to fix their minds and not their genitalia," he stated, adding that "to provide a surgical alteration to the body of these unfortunate people was to collaborate with a mental disorder rather than to treat it."

Landolt noted that the committee hearings ended in confusion over the terminology presented in the bill, and that even the bill's sponsor, NDP MP [New Democratic Party Member of Parliament] Randall Garrison, was not clear as to who is included and who is excluded in these terms.

"The definition for 'gender identity' proposed by Mr. Garrison is a subjective one that he defined as a 'deeply felt internal and individual experience of gender, which may or may not correspond with the sex that the individual was assigned at birth,'" Landolt said, adding that "The committee engaged in extensive discussions on the meaning of 'gender identity' and 'gender expression' without much clarification."

Legislation Is Harmful

"As a result, instead of a smooth, orderly dispatch of this bill through the Committee orchestrated by Garrison, Conservative MP Shelly Glover (St. Boniface, Manitoba) and Conservative MP Kerry-Lynne Findlay (Delta-Richmond-East, BC [British Columbia, Canada]), the committee hearings broke down in confusion at the final hearing on December 10th [2012]. The result is that the bill will be reported to the House of Commons as originally written without amendments," Landolt stated.

Following this state of confusion over terms at the review committee, REAL Women sought out an expert in order to provide the scientific and medical evidence relating to "transgenderism" and the other terms used in the bill.

Gwen Landolt told LifeSiteNews that REAL Women of Canada will be including Dr. Berger's statement in an information package to be sent to MPs before the bill comes to final vote.

"It is crucial that MPs know that this legislation is harmful, not only to those who think themselves transgendered but also to society, and should not be passed into law," Landolt said. "We must therefore write to our MP's to request that they speak against this troubling bill."

4

Transgender People Face Widespread Discrimination

Jaime M. Grant et al.

Jaime M. Grant is the founding executive director of the Arcus Center for Social Justice Leadership (ACSJL) at Kalamazoo College in Michigan, where she is also an assistant professor.

In 2011, the National Center for Transgender Equality and the National Gay and Lesbian Task Force teamed up to do a study of 6,450 transgender and gender non-conforming people from all fifty states. The report's findings highlight the severity of discrimination and bias that trans people routinely face in all areas of their lives. Such a constant and "catastrophic" level of discrimination means transgender people are more likely to live in extreme poverty, attempt suicide, be unemployed, face homelessness, be denied medical care, experience harassment and sexual assault, or be disrespected by public officials than their non-trans peers. The pattern of abuse and injustice against trans people is systemic and deeply entrenched.

This study [National Transgender Discrimination Survey] brings to light what is both patently obvious and far too often dismissed from the human rights agenda. Transgender and gender non-conforming people face injustice at every turn: in childhood homes, in school systems that promise to shelter and educate, in harsh and exclusionary workplaces, at the grocery store, the hotel front desk, in doctors' offices and emergency rooms, before judges and at the hands of land-lords, police officers, health care workers and other service providers.

The National Gay and Lesbian Task Force and the Na-tional Center for Transgender Equality are grateful to each of the 6,450 transgender and gender non-conforming study par-ticipants who took the time and energy to answer questions about the depth and breadth of injustice in their lives. A di-verse set of people, from all 50 states, the District of Colum-bia, Puerto Rico, Guam and the U.S. Virgin Islands, completed online or paper surveys [in 2011]. This tremendous gift has created the first 360-degree picture of discrimination against transgender and gender non-conforming people in the U.S. and provides critical data points for policymakers, community activists and legal advocates to confront the appalling realities documented here and press the case for equity and justice.

Dramatic Findings

Hundreds of dramatic findings on the impact of anti-transgender bias are presented in this report. In many cases, a series of bias-related events lead to insurmountable challenges and devastating outcomes for study participants. Several meta-findings are worth noting from the outset:

- Discrimination was pervasive throughout the entire sample, yet the combination of anti-transgender bias and persistent, structural racism was especially devastating. People of color in general fare worse than white participants across the board, with Afri-can American transgender respondents faring worse than all others in many areas examined.

- Respondents lived in extreme poverty. Our sample was nearly four times more likely to have a house-hold income of less than $10,000/year compared to the general populations.

- A staggering 41% of respondents reported attempting suicide compared to 1.6% of the general population, with rates rising for those who lost a job due to bias (55%), were harassed/bullied in school (51%), had low household income, or were the victim of physical assault (61%) or sexual assault (64%).

- [In addition,] those who expressed a transgender identity or gender non-conformity while in grades K-12 reported alarming rates of harassment (78%), physical assault (35%) and sexual violence (12%); harassment was so severe that it led almost one-sixth (15%) to leave a school in K-12 settings or in higher education.

- Respondents who have been harassed and abused by teachers in K-12 settings showed dramatically worse health and other outcomes than those who did not experience such abuse. Peer harassment and abuse also had highly damaging effects.

Employment Discrimination and Economic Insecurity

• *Double the rate of unemployment*: Survey respondents experienced unemployment at twice the rate of the general population at the time of the survey, with rates for people of color up to four times the national unemployment rate.

• *Widespread mistreatment at work*: Ninety percent (90%) of those surveyed reported experiencing harassment, mistreatment or discrimination on the job or took actions like hiding who they are to avoid it.

• Forty-seven percent (47%) said they had experienced an adverse job outcome, such as being fired, not hired or denied a promotion because of being transgender or gender non-conforming.

• Over one-quarter (26%) reported that they had lost a job due to being transgender or gender non-conforming and 50% were harassed.

• Large majorities attempted to avoid discrimination by hiding their gender or gender transition (71%) or delaying their gender transition (57%).

• The vast majority (78%) of those who transitioned from one gender to the other reported that they felt more comfortable at work and their job performance improved, despite high levels of mistreatment.

• Overall, 16% said they had been compelled to work in the underground economy for income (such as doing sex work or selling drugs).

• Respondents who were currently unemployed experienced debilitating negative outcomes, including nearly double the rate of working in the underground economy (such as doing sex work or selling drugs), twice the homelessness, 85% more incarceration, and more negative health outcomes, such as more than double the HIV infection rate and nearly double the rate of current drinking or drug misuse to cope with mistreatment, compared to those who were employed.

• Respondents who had lost a job due to bias also experienced ruinous consequences such as four times the rate of homelessness, 70% more current drinking or misuse of drugs to cope with mistreatment, 85% more incarceration, more than double the rate working in the underground economy, and more than double the HIV infection rate, compared to those who did not lose a job due to bias.

Housing Discrimination and Homelessness

• Respondents reported various forms of direct housing discrimination—19% reported having been refused a home or apartment and 11% reported being evicted because of their gender identity/expression.

• One-fifth (19%) reported experiencing homelessness at some point in their lives because they were transgender or gender non-conforming; the majority of those trying to access a homeless shelter were harassed by shelter staff or residents (55%), 29% were turned away altogether, and 22% were sexually assaulted by residents or staff.

• Almost 2% of respondents were currently homeless, which is almost twice the rate of the general population (1%).

• Respondents reported less than half the national rate of home ownership: 32% reported owning their home compared to 67% of the general population.

• Respondents who have experienced homelessness were highly vulnerable to mistreatment in public settings, police abuse and negative health outcomes.

• Fifty-three percent (53%) of respondents reported being verbally harassed or disrespected in a place of public accommodation, including hotels, restaurants, buses, airports and government agencies.

• Respondents experienced widespread abuse in the public sector, and were often abused at the hands of "helping" professionals and government officials. One fifth (22%) were denied equal treatment by a government agency or official; 29% reported police harassment or disrespect; and 12% had been denied equal treatment or harassed by judges or court officials.

Legal Interactions

• Of those who have transitioned gender, only one-fifth (21%) have been able to update *all* of their IDs [identification cards] and records with their new gender. One-third (33%) of those who had transitioned had updated *none* of their IDs/records.

• Only 59% reported updating the gender on their driver's license/state ID, meaning 41% live without ID that matches their gender identity.

• Forty percent (40%) of those who presented ID (when it was required in the ordinary course of life) that did not match their gender identity/expression reported being harassed, 3% reported being attacked or assaulted, and 15% reported being asked to leave.

• One-fifth (22%) of respondents who have interacted with police reported harassment by police, with much higher rates reported by people of color.

• Almost half of the respondents (46%) reported being uncomfortable seeking police assistance.

• Physical and sexual assault in jail/prison is a serious problem: 16% of respondents who had been to jail or prison reported being physically assaulted and 15% reported being sexually assaulted.

Discrimination in Health Care and Poor Health Outcomes

• Health outcomes for all categories of respondents show the appalling effects of social and economic marginalization, including much higher rates of HIV infection, smoking, drug and alcohol use and suicide attempts than the general population.

• *Refusal of care*: 19% of our sample reported being refused medical care due to their transgender or gender non-conforming status, with even higher numbers among people of color in the survey.

• *Uninformed doctors*: 50% of the sample reported having to teach their medical providers about transgender care.

• *High HIV rates*: Respondents reported over four times the national average of HIV infection, with rates higher among transgender people of color.

• *Postponed care*: Survey participants reported that when they were sick or injured, many postponed medical care due to discrimination (28%) or inability to afford it (48%).

Family Acceptance and Resilience

• Forty-three percent (43%) maintained most of their family bonds, while 57% experienced significant family rejection.

• In the face of extensive institutional discrimination, family acceptance had a protective affect against many threats to well-being including health risks such as HIV infection and suicide. Families were more likely to remain together and provide support for transgender and gender nonconforming family members than stereotypes suggest.

Society blames transgender and gender non-conforming people for bringing the discrimination and violence on themselves.

Despite all of the harassment, mistreatment, discrimination and violence faced by respondents, study participants also demonstrated determination, resourcefulness and perseverance.

• Although the survey identified major structural barriers to obtaining health care, 76% of transgender respondents have been able to receive hormone therapy, indicating a determination to endure the abuse or search out sensitive medical providers.

• Despite high levels of harassment, bullying and violence in school, many respondents were able to obtain an education by returning to school. Although fewer 18 to 24-year-olds were currently in school compared to the general population, respondents returned to school in large numbers at later ages, with 22% of those aged 25–44 currently in school (compared to 7% of the general population).

• Over three-fourths (78%) reported feeling more comfortable at work and their performance improving after transitioning, despite reporting nearly the same rates of harassment at work as the overall sample.

• Of the 26% who reported losing a job due to bias, 58% reported being currently employed and of the 19% who reported facing housing discrimination in the form of a denial of a home/apartment, 94% reported being currently housed.

Cumulative Discrimination

Sixty-three percent (63%) of our participants had experienced a serious act of discrimination—events that would have a major impact on a person's quality of life and ability to sustain themselves financially or emotionally. These events included the following:

• Lost job due to bias

• Eviction due to bias

• School bullying/harassment so severe the respondent had to drop out

• Teacher bullying

• Physical assault due to bias

• Sexual assault due to bias

• Homelessness because of gender identity/expression

• Lost relationship with partner or children due to gender identity/expression

• Denial of medical service due to bias

• Incarceration due to gender identity/expression

Almost a quarter (23%) of our respondents experienced a catastrophic level of discrimination—having been impacted by at least three of the above major life-disrupting events due to bias. These compounding acts of discrimination—due to the prejudice of others or lack of protective laws—exponentially increase the difficulty of bouncing back and establishing a stable economic and home life.

A Systemic Problem

It is part of social and legal convention in the United States to discriminate against, ridicule, and abuse transgender and gender non-conforming people within foundational institutions such as the family, schools, the workplace and health care settings, every day. Instead of recognizing that the moral failure lies in society's unwillingness to embrace different gender identities and expressions, society blames transgender and gender non-conforming people for bringing the discrimination and violence on themselves.

Nearly every system and institution in the United States, both large and small, from local to national, is implicated by this data. Medical providers and health systems, government agencies, families, businesses and employers, schools and colleges, police departments, jail and prison systems—each of these systems and institutions is failing daily in its obligation to serve transgender and gender non-conforming people, instead subjecting them to mistreatment ranging from commonplace disrespect to outright violence, abuse and the denial of human dignity. The consequences of these widespread injustices are human and real, ranging from unemployment and homelessness to illness and death.

This report is a call to action for all of us, especially for those who pass laws and set policies and practices, whose action or continued inaction will make a significant difference between the current climate of discrimination and violence and a world of freedom and equality. And everyone else, from those who drive buses or teach our children to those who sit on the judicial bench or write prescriptions, must also take up the call for human rights for transgender and gender non-conforming people, and confront this pattern of abuse and injustice.

We must accept nothing less than a complete elimination of this pervasive inhumanity; we must work continuously and strenuously together for justice.

5

Transgender People Need More Legal Protection

Movement Advancement Project et al.

The Movement Advancement Project (MAP) is an independent think tank that collaborates with LGBT (lesbin, gay, bisexual, and transgender) organizations to provide information, analysis, and resources that advance their efforts. This viewpoint was authored by MAP and the Center for American Progress, the Human Rights Campaign, and the National Center for Transgender Equality.

Transgender employees routinely face discrimination in the workplace, including bias in hiring and firing, wage inequities, insufficient legal protections, unequal access to health coverage, denial of personal medical leave, and general harassment and discrimination because of who they are. Such inequities translate to especially high rates of unemployment and poverty among transgender Americans. Legal protections for transgender workers should be enacted on the local, state, and federal levels.

Editor's Note: On July 21, 2014, President Barack Obama signed an executive order prohibiting the federal government and businesses that hold federal contracts from discriminating against workers on the basis of sexual orientation or transgender status. The order adds gender identity to a long-standing list of protected groups for the first time. Obama has said he hopes Congress will enact a similar law for all employers in order to protect LGBT workers nationwide.

The basic American bargain is that people who work hard and meet their responsibilities should be able to get ahead. It is an agreement that workers will be judged and rewarded based on their contributions and capabilities—no matter who they are, what they look like, or where they are from. This basic bargain is not just an idea—it is embedded in laws that promote equal access to jobs and that protect workers from unfair practices.

For transgender workers in America, this bargain is broken. Instead of having a fair chance to get ahead, transgender workers often are held back by bias and unequal workplace benefits. Even though 77% of voters say they support protecting transgender people from discrimination in employment, no federal law provides explicit legal protections for transgender workers based on gender identity/expression; and only 17 states and the District of Columbia have laws that offer these protections.

Among the results of these inequities are extraordinarily high rates of unemployment and poverty among transgender people in the United States.

Transgender Workers in America

A 2011 analysis by the Williams Institute estimates that 0.3% of American adults, or 700,000 Americans, are transgender. The report presents the latest demographic information about transgender workers, including:

- The population of transgender workers is expected to grow. More younger people are identifying as lesbian, gay, bisexual and transgender (LGBT). A 2012 Gallup poll found that, compared with older adults, a much greater proportion of young people identify as LGBT: 6.4% of adults between the ages of 18 and 29 self-identify as LGBT, compared to 1.9% of adults age 65+.

- Transgender workers are geographically dispersed. Respondents in the National Transgender Discrimination Survey lived in all 50 states, and their geographic distribution approximately mirrored that of the general U.S. population.

- Transgender workers are racially and ethnically diverse. The National Transgender Discrimination Survey found that 24% of transgender people in the U.S. identified as people of color, compared to 22% of the general population. Also, 4% of transgender adults are immigrants.

- Transgender people are highly educated. Transgender respondents to the National Transgender Discrimination Survey had much higher levels of educational attainment than the population as a whole, with 87% of transgender people reporting that they had at least some college and 47% reporting that they had obtained a college or graduate degree.

Transgender employees face wage disparities that make it harder for them to provide for themselves and their families.

- Employment discrimination and the impact of social stigma contribute to very high rates of unemployment among transgender workers. The National Transgender Discrimination Survey found that the unemployment rate for transgender workers was twice the rate for the population as a whole (14% compared to 7%), with the rate for transgender people of color reaching as high as four times the national unemployment rate.

- High rates of unemployment and underemployment place transgender people at extraordinarily high risk of poverty. According to the National Transgender

Discrimination Survey, transgender people are nearly four times more likely to have a household income under $10,000 per year than the population as a whole (15% vs. 4%).

Discrimination with Limited Legal Protection

For many transgender workers in the United States, going to work still means facing harassment, discrimination and unjust firing without explicit legal protection. The report summarizes four discrimination-related barriers facing transgender workers.

Barrier #1: Pervasive Misunderstanding, Hiring Bias and On-The-Job Discrimination. Many Americans have very little understanding of what it means to be transgender. As a result, for transgender people seeking work, the entire job search and hiring process is a minefield, particularly if a legal name or gender on an identity document does not match the outward appearance of the applicant. Once a transgender employee is hired, he or she may face many forms of harassment and discrimination, including denial of promotions or unfair firing.

Barrier #2: Wage Inequities. In addition to job and workplace discrimination, transgender employees face wage disparities that make it harder for them to provide for themselves and their families.

Barrier #3: Unclear Legal Protections. Transgender workers may seek federal legal recourse by filing a complaint with the Equal Employment Opportunity Commission (EEOC) for sex discrimination under Title VII of the Civil Rights Act. But federal law does not provide explicit nondiscrimination protections for transgender workers, and only 17 states and the District of Columbia explicitly prohibit discrimination based on gender identity/expression.

Barrier #4: Inability to Update Legal Documents. Historically, state and federal governments have imposed intrusive and burdensome requirements—such as proof of sex reassignment surgery—that have made it impossible for many transgender people to obtain accurate and consistent identification documents. When these documents do not match a transgender individual's gender presentation, it can greatly complicate that person's life, particularly in a post-9/11 [terrorist attacks of September 11, 2001] world.

Inequitable Health and Leave Benefits

For most workers in the United States, a paycheck is only one of many important benefits that come with having a job. Other work-related benefits include health insurance and family and medical leave. The report describes in detail how the denial of health and leave benefits for many transgender workers results in health problems, added costs for medical care and other problems.

> *Fair-minded employers who want to do what they can to treat all their workers fairly and equally can also make changes to their health insurance and leave policies to ensure that transgender workers are treated fairly.*

Barrier #5: Unequal Access to Health Insurance Benefits. Although transgender employees may have equal access to health insurance enrollment, they may still be denied appropriate coverage and care. For example, a transgender employee may find that an insurance company refuses to cover a range of routine and medically necessary care because of coverage exclusions that directly or inadvertently target transgender people. Exclusions in health insurance often deny transgender workers access to both basic healthcare and transition-related care.

Barrier #6: Denial of Personal Medical Leave. Employers may deny transgender workers leave for transition-related care, incorrectly stating that such care does not constitute a "serious medical condition." As a result, transgender employees may face a difficult choice: Put their jobs at risk to care for themselves, or make do without leave and put their health in jeopardy.

Policy Recommendations

The report offers detailed recommendations for action to fix the broken bargain for transgender workers by the federal, state and local governments, as well as employers. The following is a summary of these recommendations:

Eliminating or reducing bias, discrimination and wage gaps for transgender workers. The report includes recommendations for strengthening workplace protections at the federal, state and local levels—as well as recommendations for partnering with employers to develop strong policies and practices to foster diverse and inclusive workplaces, regardless of the law. Major recommendations include:

Federal Solutions

- Congress should ban public and private employment discrimination nationwide on the basis of gender identity/expression and sexual orientation.

- The President should mandate that federal contractors prohibit discrimination on the basis of gender identity/expression and sexual orientation.

- The federal government and its agencies should work to make it easier for transgender people to update their identity documents to match their lived gender.

State and Local Solutions

- State lawmakers should ban employment discrimination in states without current protections for gender identity/expression.

- Governors should mandate that state employers and contractors prohibit discrimination on the basis of gender identity/expression.

- In the absence of nationwide and state-level protections, local lawmakers should take action to protect transgender workers.

Employer Solutions

- Employers should send a clear message that workplace discrimination against transgender workers will not be tolerated.

- Employers should dispel myths/stereotypes and increase awareness through workforce diversity training.

- Employers should ensure support for transitioning transgender employees.

Eliminating Inequitable Health and Leave Benefits

Equitable access to health and leave benefits for transgender workers requires action by federal, state, and local policymakers. However, fair-minded employers who want to do what they can to treat all their workers fairly and equally can also make changes to their health insurance and leave policies to ensure that transgender workers are treated fairly on the job. The report includes recommendations related to both health insurance and medical leave for transgender workers. Among the major recommendations:

Health Insurance

- The U.S. Department of Health and Human Services should continue to clarify and enforce nondiscrimination protections covering transgender people under the Affordable Care Act.

- State lawmakers and/or policymakers should revise state insurance laws and/or policies to ensure that LGBT workers can obtain individual health insurance (whether purchased privately or provided through employers) that meets their healthcare needs.

- Federal, state and local lawmakers should extend equal health benefits to all government employees, including transgender workers.

- Employers should offer affordable health insurance benefits, including routine and transition-related care, for transgender employees.

Medical Leave

- The Department of Labor should clarify that the federal Family and Medical Leave Act (FMLA) allows leave for transgender workers seeking transition-related care.

- State lawmakers and/or policymakers should revise or pass state medical and family leave laws and policies to explicitly include transgender workers.

- Employers should expand leave options beyond existing state and federal mandates.

Fixing the broken bargain for transgender workers will help ensure that they are treated fairly no matter where they work, that they receive the same compensation for the same work, and that they can access important benefits available to other workers to protect their health and livelihood. It is time to send transgender workers the message that they matter, and to show that our nation and our economy are stronger when we treat all workers fairly.

6

Giving Transgender People Special Legal Status Is Bad Public Policy

Ryan T. Anderson

Ryan T. Anderson researches and writes about marriage and religious liberty as the William E. Simon fellow at the Heritage Foundation, a conservative think tank based in Washington, DC.

Americans should oppose discrimination and bias, but the proposed Employment Non-Discrimination Act of 2013 (ENDA) constitutes unacceptable government interference in the marketplace and threatens the fundamental First Amendment rights of religious freedom and free speech. By including protections for transgender people based on the changeable concept of "gender identity," ENDA creates a special new protected class that is ambiguously defined and which is ripe for abuse. ENDA would prohibit employers from considering the consequences of transgenderism in their workplace, ban decisions based on an employer's moral beliefs, and would weaken marriage culture overall. Fearing violation of ENDA, employers would be hesitant to lay off transgender workers and the law could discourage overall hiring; the economic impact of lawsuits could be substantial. Gender-identity protection laws like ENDA are bad public policy.

Editor's Note: ENDA was approved by the US Senate on November 7, 2013 on a bipartisan vote of 64-32. By late July 2014, the bill had been referred to the House of Representatives Sub-

committee on Workforce Protections but had not been brought to the House floor for a vote. Republican Speaker of the House John Boehner opposes ENDA and has said there is "no way" it will pass in the current session of Congress.

America is dedicated to protecting First Amendment freedoms while respecting citizens' equality before the law. None of these freedoms is absolute: Strong governmental interests can at times trump fundamental civil liberties. But the Employment Non-Discrimination Act of 2013 (ENDA) does not satisfy any such interest; rather, it tramples First Amendment rights and unnecessarily impinges on citizens' right to run their businesses the way they choose. The proposed legislation does not protect equality before the law; instead it would create special privileges that are enforceable against private actors.

ENDA [Employment Non-Discrimination Act of 2013] defines "gender identity" as "the gender-related identity, appearance, or mannerisms or other gender-related characteristics of an individual, with or without regard to the individual's designated sex at birth."

ENDA could also have serious unintended consequences. It would impose liability on employers for alleged "discrimination" based not on objective employee traits, but on subjective and unverifiable identities. ENDA would further increase government interference in labor markets, potentially discouraging job creation. It does not provide adequate protections for religious liberty or freedom of speech. Finally, especially related to issues surrounding "gender identity" and "transgender" employees, this law could require employment policies that, with regard to a number of workplace conditions, undermine common sense.

In short, ENDA seeks to regulate employment decisions that are best handled by private actors without federal government interference. ENDA disregards the consciences and liberties of people of goodwill who happen not to share the government's opinions about issues of marriage and sexuality.

Of course employers should respect the intrinsic dignity of all of their employees, but ENDA is bad public policy. Its threats to our freedoms unite civil libertarians concerned about free speech and religious liberty, free marketers concerned about freedom of contract and government interference in the marketplace, and social conservatives concerned about marriage and culture:

ENDA 2013: A Primer

ENDA creates special privileges based on sexual orientation and gender identity. Specifically, it would make it illegal for organizations with 15 or more employees to "fail or refuse to hire or to discharge any individual, or otherwise discriminate against any individual with respect to the compensation, terms, conditions, or privileges of employment of the individual, because of such individual's actual or perceived sexual orientation or gender identity."

ENDA defines "sexual orientation" as "homosexuality, heterosexuality, or bisexuality" but offers no definition of those terms or what principle limits "orientation" to those three. Likewise, ENDA defines "gender identity" as "the gender-related identity, appearance, or mannerisms or other gender-related characteristics of an individual, with or without regard to the individual's designated sex at birth." In other words, unlike previous versions of the bill, ENDA's current incarnation now creates special rights for transgendered individuals— males who dress and act as females and females who dress and act as males—and forbids employers from considering the consequences of such behavior at the workplace.

ENDA does not contain a Bona Fide Occupational Qualification (BFOQ) exemption. BFOQs, which some other employment laws contain, allow employers to make employment decisions that could otherwise constitute discrimination so long as those decisions are honestly related to job qualifications. For example, Title VII of the Civil Rights Act contains a BFOQ that allows employers to take sex into account: hiring a female camp counselor at an all-girls sleep-away summer camp, for example, or hiring men or women at jobs that would be particularly dangerous or difficult for members of one or another sex. ENDA has no provision that would protect those jobs where one's sexual orientation or gender identity is a bona fide occupational qualification that is reasonably connected to the mission of the business and the responsibilities of the job. . . .

The Subjectivity of Gender Identity

Some argue that the market is not able to protect the interests of employees sufficiently and that the government must therefore intervene, as it did with issues of race and sex, but the argument that prohibiting so-called discrimination on the basis of sexual orientation and gender identity is akin to prohibiting actual discrimination on the basis of sex or race is misguided. Sexual orientation and gender identity differ in several important respects from race or sex. . . .

While race is usually readily apparent, the groups seeking special status in ENDA are not defined by objective characteristics. Sexual orientation and gender identity are commonly understood to be subjective, self-disclosed, and self-defined. And unlike race, sexual orientation and gender identity are usually understood to include behaviors. An employer's decisions reasonably taking into account the behavior of employees are core personnel decisions best left to businesses themselves, not to the federal government.

Paul McHugh, MD, University Distinguished Service Professor of Psychiatry at the Johns Hopkins University School of Medicine, and Gerard V. Bradley, Professor of Law at the University of Notre Dame, explain:

[S]ocial science research continues to show that sexual orientation, unlike race, color, and ethnicity, is neither a clearly defined concept nor an immutable characteristic of human beings. Basing federal employment law on a vaguely defined concept such as sexual orientation, especially when our courts have a wise precedent of limiting suspect classes to groups that have a clearly-defined shared characteristic, would undoubtedly cause problems for many well-meaning employers.

No Scientific Consensus

McHugh and Bradley caution against elevating sexual orientation and gender identity to the status of protected characteristics because of the lack of clear definition:

> "Sexual orientation" should not be recognized as a newly protected characteristic of individuals under federal law. And neither should "gender identity" or any cognate concept. In contrast with other characteristics, it is neither discrete nor immutable. There is no scientific consensus on how to define sexual orientation, and the various definitions proposed by experts produce substantially different groups of peopled.

Indeed, there is no clear scientific evidence that sexual orientation and gender identity are biologically determined. McHugh and Bradley summarize the relevant scholarly scientific research on sexual orientation and gender identity:

> Nor is there any convincing evidence that sexual orientation is biologically determined; rather, research tends to show that for some persons and perhaps for a great many, "sexual orientation" is plastic and fluid; that is, it changes over time. What we do know with certainty about sexual orientation is that it is affective and behavioral—a matter of desire and/or behavior. And "gender identity" is even more fluid and erratic, so much so that in limited cases an individual could claim to "identify" with a different gender on successive days

at work. Employers should not be obliged by dint of civil and possibly criminal penalties to adjust their workplaces to suit felt needs such as these.

Because sexual orientation and gender identity are subjective concepts that may change over time, a law invoking them to define a protected class would be especially ripe for abuse. For instance, employees who are dismissed for legitimate reasons might afterward claim that their employer fired them because its perceptions of their sexual orientation or gender identity changed.

Under ENDA, employers could become more reluctant to hire such "protected class" employees in the first place.

Economic Consequences

ENDA would create serious problems for employers seeking to manage their businesses while complying with the law. . . .

Limiting the ability to lay off dissuades employers from hiring. ENDA would chip away at the at-will employment doctrine that has made the American labor market so much stronger than European labor markets.

The subjective nature of sexual orientation and gender identity magnifies these problems by giving employees carte blanche to threaten a lawsuit against their employer in response to adverse employment actions. Further, under the Supreme Court's interpretation of Title VII, employers must pay plaintiffs' attorney's fees if they lose an anti-discrimination suit, but they may not recover attorney's fees from unsuccessful plaintiffs unless they can prove that the suit was groundless—a high bar to clear.

The legal cost of successfully defending a case at trial typically runs into hundreds of thousands of dollars. This one-way ratchet strongly discourages companies from laying off employees who could file plausible anti-discrimination suits, and it acts as an incentive for disgruntled or former employees to file suits. Consequently, under ENDA, employers could become more reluctant to hire such "protected class" employees in the first place. . . .

Compounding these legal problems is the fact that sexual orientation and gender identity are unclear, ambiguous terms. They can refer to voluntary behaviors as well as thoughts and inclinations, and it is reasonable for employers to make distinctions based on actions. Consequently, ENDA would prohibit reasonable decisions to base employment on behavior. . . .

A Threat to Religious Liberty and Speech

One of ENDA's most concerning implications: The law would further weaken the marriage culture and the ability of citizens and their associations to affirm that marriage is the union of a man and a woman and that sexual relations are reserved for marriage so understood. ENDA would treat these convictions as if they were bigotry.

Furthermore, ENDA would ban decisions based on moral views common to the Abrahamic faith traditions and to great thinkers from Plato to Kant as unjust discrimination. Whether by religion, reason, or experience, many people of goodwill believe that our bodies are an essential part of who we are. On this view, maleness and femaleness are not arbitrary constructs but objective ways of being human to be valued and affirmed, not rejected or altered. Thus, our sexual embodiment as male and female goes to the heart of what marriage is: a union of sexually complementary spouses. Again, however, ENDA would deem such judgments irrational and unlawful.

ENDA could also stifle speech in the workplace. For example, as Hans Bader notes, the Supreme Court found that Title VII "require[s] employers to prohibit employee speech or conduct that creates a 'hostile or offensive work environment' for women, blacks, or religious minorities." Employers may even be on the hook for damages and attorney's fees if they were negligent in failing to notice, stop, or discipline employees whose speech or conduct creates such an environment. ENDA would extend these restrictions to "actual and perceived sexual orientation or gender identity."

Consequently, employees or employers who express disapproving religious or political views of same-sex behavior could potentially create enormous legal liabilities. Businesses would likely respond to such potential liability by self-censoring their speech and preventing employees from expressing views such as support for marriage as a union of one man and one woman: In essence, ENDA really would become a "general civility code" far beyond the scope of Title VII. . . .

Inadequate Protections

ENDA also raises serious religious liberty concerns, especially for morally traditional religious communities and religious citizens who operate in the marketplace. While ENDA provides some religious liberty protections, they are inadequate and vaguely denned. . . .

While it is unclear which religious organizations would be exempted from ENDA, it is clear that the bill would not exempt those who wish to run their businesses and other organizations in keeping with their moral or religious values.

Prohibiting employers from making decisions about transgendered employees, especially when in positions of role-modeling, could be detrimental to children and to workplace morale.

Additionally, ENDA's religious liberty protections extend only to businesses directly run by a church or religious organizations. As a result, other religious business owners would be exposed to significant liabilities. Consider, for instance, a Christian bookstore not formally incorporated as a religious organization. Such a store could be accused of creating a hostile work environment by selling and promoting books stating that marriage unites one man with one woman.

Clearly, ENDA would create enormous legal risks for businesses that allowed their employees to express traditional religious teachings on sexuality. Anti-discrimination law ought not to silence religious believers.

In truth, it is hard to square ENDA's basic purpose with any robust protection of citizens' rights to speak freely about their religious or moral convictions about marriage and sexuality. Indeed, Americans are paying the price when their state or local governments have passed sexual orientation and gender identity statutes.

Unintended Detrimental Consequences

The enforcement of ENDA could also have harmful unintended consequences, especially with regard to the inclusion of gender identity. Prohibiting employers from making decisions about transgendered employees, especially when in positions of role-modeling, could be detrimental to children and to workplace morale.

First, it is important to recognize that issues of sex and gender identity are psychologically, morally, and politically fraught, but all should agree that children should be protected from having to sort through such questions before an age-appropriate introduction. ENDA would prevent employers from protecting children from these adult debates about sex and gender identity by barring employers from making certain decisions about transgendered employees.

Second, ENDA could provide some exemptions for religious education, but it provides no protection for students in other schools who would be prematurely exposed to questions about sex and gender if a male teacher returned to school identifying as a woman.

Finally, whatever the significance of gender identity, society cannot deny the relevance, in many contexts, of biological sex. For example, an employer would be negligent to ignore the concerns of female employees about having to share bathrooms with a biological male who identifies as female. Failing to do so raises a host of concerns about privacy rights. Indeed, state laws are already creating such concerns. As Bader reports:

> ENDA also contains "transgender rights" provisions that ban discrimination based on "gender identity." Similar prohibitions in state laws created legal headaches for some businesses. One case pitted a transgender employee with male DNA who sued after being denied permission to use the ladies' restroom, a denial that resulted from complaints filed by female employees. The employer lost in the Minnesota Court of Appeals, but then prevailed in the Minnesota Supreme Court. Another case involved a male-looking person who sued and obtained a substantial settlement after being ejected from the ladies' room in response to complaints by a female customer who thought that a man had just invaded the ladies' room. . . .

There is no limiting principle for what will be classified as a sexual orientation or gender identity in the future.

Ultimately, McHugh and Bradley conclude that ENDA would "lead to insurmountable enforcement difficulties, arbitrary and even whimsical results in many cases, and it would have an unjustified chilling effect upon all too many employers' decisions." Allowing employers to make decisions based on their employees' behavior, including their sexual and gender-identity behavior, is good policy, but ENDA would eliminate it.

Bad Public Policy

All citizens should oppose unjust discrimination, but ENDA is not the way to achieve that goal. ENDA threatens fundamental First Amendment rights. It creates new, subjective protected classes that leave employers guessing about how to comply with the law and opens them to unimaginable liability. ENDA would also increase government interference in the labor markets in ways that could harm the economy.

Additionally, ENDA would further weaken the marriage culture and the freedom of citizens and their associations to affirm their religious or moral convictions, such as that marriage is the union of one man and one woman and that sexual relations are reserved for marriage so understood. ENDA could ban employment decisions based on the moral and religious beliefs of private employers. Many people of goodwill believe that our bodies are an essential part of who we are, that maleness and femaleness are to be valued and affirmed. ENDA would treat expressing these beliefs in an employment context as actionable discrimination.

ENDA would limit the ability of private employers to run their own businesses and is an unjust assault on the consciences and liberties of people of goodwill who happen not to share the government's opinions about issues of marriage and sexuality. Employers should respect the intrinsic dignity of all of their employees, but ENDA is not the right policy to realize that goal. Whether you care about civil liberties, market economies, traditional values, or all three—as this author does—it is important to see that ENDA is bad public policy.

7

The Transgender Rights Movement Is Fighting for Equality

Associated Press

The Associated Press is a news wire service.

The transgender rights movement has experienced some important legal and political victories recently but still faces substantial obstacles in building public support for its cause. Trans advocates say the strong backlash now coming from conservative and religious groups is a sign that transgender people are making real progress and are now "on the radar" so the trans community's unique concerns and needs can finally get the attention they deserve. The key to winning acceptance and gaining support, advocates say, is for transgender people to be more visible in society so Americans can become more familiar with them.

Editor's Note: By late July 2014, the Employment Nondiscrimination Act of 2013 (ENDA) had been referred to the House of Representatives Subcommittee on Workforce Protections but was unlikely to be brought to the House floor for a vote during the current session of Congress.

As gays and lesbians rack up victories in their quest for marriage equality and other rights, transgender Americans are following in their path—hopefully, but less smoothly.

There have been some important legal rulings and political votes in recent months bolstering transgender rights. But those have coincided with an upsurge of hostility from some conservative activists and an acknowledgement by transgender-rights leaders that they face distinct challenges in building public support for their cause.

"My sense is that we are 20 years behind the mainstream gay and lesbian movement in terms of public understanding," said Michael Silverman, executive director of the Transgender Legal Defense and Education Fund.

"I see a lessening of anti-gay rhetoric as the American people get to know gays and lesbians," he said. "But fewer Americans know transgender people that way at this point, and that presents an opening that opponents of transgender rights can exploit."

One high point for transgender activists came in November [2013] when the U.S. Senate approved the Employment Non-Discrimination Act, which would ban workplace discrimination on the basis of gender identity as well as sexual orientation. Only 17 states have such protections for transgender people.

Students as young as 5 or 6 years old will be forced to watch should their teacher choose to transform herself from Marvin to Mary.

However, House Speaker John Boehner has indicated that his Republican-controlled chamber may not take up the bill, and much of the criticism directed at it by social conservative activists has focused on transgender-related matters.

"This law is about forcing Bible-believing Christians to deny their faith rather than inconvenience cross-dressing, gender-confused adults," said Rick Scarborough, chairman of Tea Party Unity.

Concerns for Students

The Rev. Louis Sheldon, chairman of the Traditional Values Coalition, evoked possible application of the bill to school hiring, asserting that "students as young as 5 or 6 years old will be forced to watch should their teacher choose to transform herself from Marvin to Mary."

Similar rhetoric has surfaced in California, where conservative groups hope to place a measure on the November 2014 ballot to repeal a new law giving transgender students the choice of playing on either boys' or girls' sports teams and allowing them to use either gender's restrooms. [The effort failed to gather enough signatures to qualify for the ballot.]

The National Organization for Marriage, which since 2007 has been a leading opponent of same-sex marriage, decided this fall to join the repeal campaign, even though the California law does not deal with marriage.

"We can stop this outrageous law in its tracks, and thwart the efforts of homosexual activists to use vulnerable children as a weapon in their culture war," wrote the organization's president, Brian Brown, in a fundraising appeal to supporters.

Repeal backers have submitted 620,000 signatures supporting a ballot measure; those are now being reviewed to see if enough of them are valid. [They were not.]

Dru Levasseur, director of Lambda Legal's Transgender Rights Project, interpreted the wave of hostile rhetoric as a positive sign.

"The fact we've had so many victories on behalf of gays and lesbians means transgender people are now on the radar—and with it comes the nastiness," he said. "There have been so many advances regarding [same-sex] marriage that the anti-equality groups are shifting to target the next set of upcoming victories on transgender issues." . . .

Pressing Issues Ignored?

For the most part, transgender activists have welcomed the developments on marriage equality, while expressing some concern that issues of more direct importance to them were not getting sufficient attention from national gay-rights groups.

Health care coverage figures among these issues. In New York state—one of the most liberal when it comes to gay rights—activists recently launched a campaign to change what they consider to be a discriminatory regulation barring Medicaid payments for purposes related to gender reassignment

Dean Spade, a transgender law professor spending this year at Columbia Law School, said other pressing issues include high rates of incarceration and poverty among transgender people, as well as violence directed against them. He has questioned why some activists are instead placing a priority on helping transgender people pursue military careers.

"We should put our energies into relieving the worst conditions placed on people," Spade said.

By any measure, there have been some significant gains for transgender Americans over the past decade, including decisions by scores of municipalities and companies to extend protections and benefits to them.

Case Law v. Public Opinion

In 2011, the 11th Circuit Court of Appeals in Atlanta overturned the firing of a Georgia legislative employee who was dismissed after telling her boss she was about to undergo sex change surgery. In June [2013], the Colorado Division of Civil Rights ruled that a suburban Colorado Springs school district had discriminated against Coy Mathis, a 6-year-old transgender girl, by preventing her from using the girls' bathroom.

Yet in the western Colorado town of Delta, a school board member suggested at a public meeting in October that use of girls' locker rooms by boys would be acceptable only if they'd been castrated. In Arizona, a Republican legislator introduced a bill this year [2013] that would have made it a crime for a transgender person to use a bathroom other than the one designated for his or her birth sex. After an outcry from advocacy groups, the measure was modified, and then withdrawn—at least for this year.

A huge number of Americans now have gay family members, gay co-workers ... but most of them don't know a transgender person.

Mara Keisling, executive director of the National Center for Transgender Equality, says the best strategy for combating such attitudes would be to enable a broad swath of Americans to become more familiar with transgender people.

"A huge number of Americans now have gay family members, gay co-workers ... but most of them don't know a transgender person, and that means we're ripe for scapegoating," Keisling said. "There are a lot of people in this country who just are ignorant about us. They hear people in authority demeaning and dehumanizing us, and they believe it."

"I think for the next few years, until transgender people are more visible, come out at work, we're still going to have a lot of ignorance out there," she said.

Demographic Challenges

Part of the challenge is demographic. According to demographer Gary Gates of the [University of California, Los Angeles] UCLA School of Law's Williams Institute, an estimated 3.4% of adults in the United States identify as lesbian, gay or bisexual, while only one-tenth that many are transgender.

One of the most prominent transgender Americans in recent months has been Chelsea Manning, the Army private previously known as Bradley Manning, who was sentenced to 35 years in prison for leaking classified material to WikiLeaks.

A day after the sentencing [in August 2013], Manning announced she wanted to live as a woman and has requested estrogen treatments that would promote breast development and other female characteristics.

Another high-profile transgender figure has surfaced on "Orange is the New Black," the hit Netflix series set in a women's prison. A transgender character, Sophia, is played empathetically by transgender actress and activist Laverne Cox.

However, that character is an exception among current offerings of TV shows and films, according to GLAAD [formerly the Gay and Lesbian Alliance Against Defamation], an advocacy group that monitors media portrayals of gays, lesbians, bisexuals and transgender people.

In a report last month, GLAAD examined 20 recent TV episodes that included transgender characters and deemed 60% of them to be negative or defamatory. Common themes, according to GLAAD, are portrayals of transgender people either as clownish or sociopathic.

"We need to get more good images in the media, so people can see us as regular people, not as predators," said Tiq Milan of GLAAD's Trans Education and Media Program.

"A Visceral Reaction"

Some conservative activists contend that many Americans will have more difficulty accepting transgender rights than gay rights.

"No matter how one feels about homosexual rights . . . there is a visceral reaction to the obvious implications of gender identity laws," wrote Mathew Staver, chairman of the conservative legal group Liberty Counsel, in an email.

"One implication is men—no matter how they appear or how they actually think or identify—being able to use women's changing rooms," he wrote. "The majority of people will not accept such laws."

Peter Sprigg, a senior fellow with the conservative Family Research Council, suggested that the visible characteristics of transgender people were problematic for some Americans.

"In many cases, transgender people are not convincing in their appearance, and therefore it may be more troubling to a lot of people," he said. "It's something people really struggle with."

However, Dru Levasseur of Lambda Legal questioned the notion that—in the court of public opinion—transgender rights was a tougher sell than gay rights. The key to winning more acceptance, he said, was a willingness by transgender people to share the stories of their lives.

"Being who you are—being brave enough to be yourself," he said. "People can relate to that."

8

The Transgender Rights Movement Is Harmful to Society

Keith Fournier

Keith Fournier is editor in chief at Catholic Online *and is a deacon at St. Stephen Martyr Parish in Chesapeake, Virginia.*

Recently enacted laws that allow children in public schools to choose which gender's sports teams they want to play on or which restrooms they want to use are part of a larger movement to force society to accept a radical interpretation of gender that is wrong and dangerous. Gender is a fixed thing, not a changeable attribute, and the idea that people can "choose" gender is a false concept. Under some new interpretations, there are as many as twenty-three distinct genders, rather than just the two—male and female—that God created. Transgender activists seek to radically restructure the social order based on false beliefs about gender. The Gender Identity Movement is harmful to society and should be stopped.

This month [July 2013] California lawmakers passed legislation which requires that restrooms in public schools, from kindergarten through the twelfth grade, no longer be limited to boys or girls, young men or young women. Students who self identify as transgendered will be able to choose which restroom they use.

The legislation also requires athletic teams in public schools to allow the student, based upon their self proclaimed gender identity, to choose their team. In other words, a girl who says she is a boy must be allowed to join the football team. A boy who says he is a girl must be able to choose to be on a girls' sports team.

This legislation is part of the movement to discard gender as a given. The enthusiastic supporters of this movement claim we somehow have the ability to choose gender. In fact, they claim it is another one of those newfound rights. In the pattern of their revolutionary agenda, they use verbal engineering to prepare the way for social and legal engineering in an effort to foist their ideology on us all.

They are on the way to compelling us to succumb to their brave new world or face the consequences. Even to raise a question as to the prudence of such a social experiment results in being verbally pilloried. It may soon bring sanctions by the State.

In a world with no givens we lose the nature of the gift of our identity as male or female.

What the Vatican Says

In an address to the Roman Curia on Thursday, December 21, 2012, Pope Emeritus Benedict XVI exposed the falsity and social danger of what is now called gender theory in the circles of the cultural revolutionaries. Here is an excerpt:

> "The Chief Rabbi of France, Gilles Bernheim, has shown in a very detailed and profoundly moving study that the attack we are currently experiencing on the true structure of the family, made up of father, mother, and child, goes much deeper. While up to now we regarded a false understanding of the nature of human freedom as one cause of the crisis

of the family, it is now becoming clear that the very notion of being—of what being human really means—is being called into question."

"He quotes the famous saying of Simone de Beauvoir: 'one is not born a woman, one becomes so' (on ne naît pas femme, on le devient). These words lay the foundation for what is put forward today under the term 'gender' as a new philosophy of sexuality. According to this philosophy, sex is no longer a given element of nature, that man has to accept and personally make sense of: it is a social role that we choose for ourselves, while in the past it was chosen for us by society."

"The profound falsehood of this theory and of the anthropological revolution contained within it is obvious. People dispute the idea that they have a nature, given by their bodily identity, which serves as a defining element of the human being. They deny their nature and decide that it is not something previously given to them, but that they make it for themselves. According to the biblical creation account, being created by God as male and female pertains to the essence of the human creature. This duality is an essential aspect of what being human is all about, as ordained by God."

"This very duality as something previously given is what is now disputed. The words of the creation account: 'male and female he created them' (Gen 1:27) no longer apply. No, what applies now is this: it was not God who created them male and female—hitherto society did this, now we decide for ourselves. Man and woman as created realities, as the nature of the human being, no longer exist. Man calls his nature into question. From now on he is merely spirit and will."

"The manipulation of nature, which we deplore today where our environment is concerned, now becomes man's fundamental choice where he himself is concerned. From now on there is only the abstract human being, who chooses for

69

himself what his nature is to be. Man and woman in their created state as complementary versions of what it means to be human are disputed. But if there is no pre-ordained duality of man and woman in creation, then neither is the family any longer a reality established by creation. Likewise, the child has lost the place he had occupied hitherto and the dignity pertaining to him."

"Bernheim shows that now, perforce, from being a subject of rights, the child has become an object to which people have a right and which they have a right to obtain. When the freedom to be creative becomes the freedom to create oneself, then necessarily the Maker himself is denied and ultimately man too is stripped of his dignity as a creature of God, as the image of God at the core of his being. The defense of the family is about man himself. And it becomes clear that when God is denied, human dignity also disappears. Whoever defends God is defending man."

An Age of Darkness

We live in an age rushing into darkness while it professes to be enlightened. Benedict was correct. His insights provide clarity in a cloud of confusion. In a world with no givens we lose the nature of the gift of our identity as male or female. As a result we are impoverished not liberated.

We regularly read stories of transgender athletes. We are repeatedly told we must accommodate the idea this idea that people can choose their gender identity. Children can even choose their gender. If they are too young to do so, then parents do it for them. The *Washington Post* recently featured an article about parents who are doing that.

Transgender activism seeks to restructure the social order to reflect the false idea that gender is malleable. A Reuters news story on March 23, 2011, entitled "Transgender New Yorkers sue over birth certificates" showed how these activists are using the Courts to enforce their cultural agenda:

"A group of transgender residents filed a lawsuit against New York City over what they say are burdensome requirements for them to change the gender on their birth certificates. The city's birth certificate requirements amount to discrimination for transgender residents, said Noah Lewis, an attorney representing the residents in the case. New York's Health Department requires residents to show proof of surgical procedures in order to change the gender status on a birth certificate.

"But the lawsuit, filed by the Transgender Legal Defense and Education Fund in state Supreme Court on behalf of three residents, said many transgender people cannot afford the surgical procedures. Instead, a note from a doctor verifying someone's transgender status should be sufficient, it said. The requirements mean many transgender people cannot get up-to-date or usable identification, Lewis said. 'This subjects them to harassment and discrimination. They can be laughed at or turned away doing everyday transactions like going to the DMV (the Department of Motor Vehicles) or applying for jobs,' he said."

"One of those suing the city, Joan Prinzivalli, said she would like to get the surgery the city requires to prove she is female but she is unable to for health reasons. 'This policy is unfair to me and to other transgender people who just want IDs [identification cards] that match who we are,' she said. City attorney Gabriel Taussig said the Health Department would review the group's concerns. 'We are very sympathetic to the petitioners' concerns and recognize that this is a complex issue,' he said."

"The Health Department must be satisfied that an applicant has completely and permanently transitioned to the acquired gender prior to the issuance of a birth certificate. Birth certificates for transgendered people in New York were an issue earlier this month when the city made an apology to a transgendered couple asked to show birth certificates when getting married because the clerk claimed they did not appear to match the people in their photo IDs. They threatened to sue because state laws do not require couples to show birth certificates when getting married."

Twenty-Three Genders?

A March, 2011 article in *Mercatornet* featured an article written by Babette Francis, the National and Overseas Coordinator of Endeavour Forum Inc., a pro-life, pro-family NGO [nongovernmental organization] which has special consultative status with the Economic and Social Council of the UN [United Nations]. The article, entitled "Gender bending: let me count the ways" revealed that gender identity activists have succeeded in pushing the Australian Human Rights Commission to recognize 23 genders.

> "In the beginning there was male and female. Soon there was homosexuality. Later there were lesbians, and much later gays, bisexuals, transgenders and queers. But anyone who thinks LGBTQ [lesbian, gay, bisexual, transgender, and queer] is the full count of contemporary sexualities is sadly out of date. For example, the transgendered have for some time been divided into those who are awaiting treatment, those [who] have had hormone treatment, those who have had hormones and surgery, and those who have had hormones and surgery but are not happy and want it all reversed."

> "Enter the Australian Human Rights Commission [AHRC] with some exciting new developments. In an extraordinary document entitled 'Protection from discrimination on the basis of sexual orientation and sex and/or gender identity', the AHRC has come up with a further list of 'genders' which they require us to recognize, and on whose behalf they want our federal government to pass anti-discrimination legislation."

> "To date (by the time you read this, the AHRC's family of sexualities may have increased and multiplied) these are:

transgender, trans, transsexual, intersex, androgynous, agender, cross dresser, drag king, drag queen, genderfluid, genderqueer, intergender, neutrois, pansexual, pan-gendered, third gender, third sex, sistergirl and brotherboy. (No, I don't know what 'neutrois' means)." [Neutrois refers to a gender identity that is genderless or agender.]

"So if we add these genders to the LGBTQ list we get 23 in all, not to mention the divisions within the transgendered group. For PR [public relations] purposes, however, the 'gendered' community now identifies itself as LGBTQI (the 'I' stands for 'intersex'.) Rather than abbreviating I think they should add all the other letters of the alphabet, then we would all feel protected and not discriminated against."

"Being Indian by birth and having married an Australian of Anglo-Celtic origin, I am all for diversity, but I am not going to commit to 'neutrois' until someone tells me what it means. Once the government passes proposed legislation, presumably businesses will be required to provide designated toilets for each gender, and Equal Opportunity Gender Identity (EOGI) units will ensure compliance with federal legislation."

Every single human cell contains chromosomes which identify whether we are male or female. That cannot be changed.

Gender Confusion Abounds

These articles reflect where this is headed unless we expose it and oppose it. The operative word in all of this is gender. Cultural revolutionaries are intent on redefining the word. Then, using the Police Power of the State, they insist that people be guaranteed a right to choose their gender and change their mind at whim.

Babette Francis mentioned a book in the gender identity movement, "Trans People in Love", co-edited by Katrina Fox, an Australian activist, who wrote an emotive piece for the Australian Broadcasting Commission recently entitled "Marriage needs redefining." In it she insists that all the "gender boundaries" surrounding marriage must be removed. "A more inclusive option," she begins, "is to allow individuals to get married whatever their sex or gender, including those who identify as having no sex or gender or whose sex may be indeterminate."

We also face an increase of what are wrongly referred to as Sex Change or Gender Reassignment surgeries. Though those who suffer from Gender Identity Disorder (GID) deserve empathy, the facts remain; no such surgery can accomplish a change of gender or sexual identity. In effect, they mutilate the body and destroy the bodily integrity of the person.

Every single human cell contains chromosomes which identify whether we are male or female. That cannot be changed. It is a given. In fact, it is a gift.

Surgery Does Not Change Gender Reality

In a culture where freedom is redefined as a right to choose anything and liberty has degenerated into license, the newspeak of the age calls the instrumental use of the body of another sexual freedom. Sadly, the same spirit of the age fails to recognize the integral unity of the human person, body, soul and spirit, and has turned the human body into a machine with parts which the revolutionaries think can simply be interchanged.

Removal of genitals and attachment of artificially constructed ones which are absolutely incapable of ovulation or conception, in the case of a transsexual male who tries to be a woman, or the generation of sperm, in the case of a transsexual woman trying to be a man, does not change the structure of reality.

The removal constitutes mutilation and the construction of artificial organs with no reproductive function does not alter the gender or sex of the person. Medical science confirms that our identity as male or female affects even our brains. In addition, even the physical appearance must be sustained by massive doses of synthetic hormones.

In 2002 the Congregation for the Doctrine of the Faith of the Catholic Church issued a letter sent without public release to every Bishop. It clearly stated that such surgical procedures do not alter a person's gender and that in no circumstance are baptismal records of such individuals who have undergone them to be altered. Further, the document made clear that no one who has undergone such a surgery is eligible to marry, be ordained to the priesthood or enter the religious life.

Exposing the Gender Identity Movement

At the time the letter was received from Rome, Bishop Wilton D. Gregory of Belleville, Ill., was the President of the U.S. Bishops' conference. He sent a letter to all US Bishops in which he wrote "The altered condition of a member of the faithful under civil law does not change one's canonical condition, which is male or female as determined at the moment of birth."

The Gender Identity Movement insists upon the recognition in the positive law of a newfound right to somehow choose one's gender. They insist upon laws which accommodate, fund, and enforce this newfound right. Those involved in the activist wing of the movement want to compel the rest of society to recognize their vision of a brave new world or face the Police Power of the State.

Pope Emeritus Benedict was correct, "the profound falsehood of this theory and of the anthropological revolution contained within it is obvious." Gender is gift: the dangers of the Gender Identity Movement must be exposed.

9

Sex-Reassignment Surgery Is a Medical Necessity

Lambda Legal

Lambda Legal, also known as the Lambda Legal Defense and Education Fund, is a civil rights organization that works to advance lesbian, gay, bisexual, and transgender (LGBT) rights through legal action, education, and public-policy advocacy.

There is broad consensus among professional organizations in the health care and mental health fields: transitioning genders is a medical necessity for many transgender people, and both public and private insurance should cover transition care such as hormone therapies and sex-reassignment surgeries. There is also broad concern about the discrimination that transgender people frequently face in health-care settings. The following viewpoint includes policy statements on transgender health from the American Medical Association, American Psychological Association, American Academy of Family Physicians, National Association of Social Workers, World Professional Association for Transgender Health, National Commission on Correctional Health Care, American Public Health Association, and American College of Obstetricians and Gynecologists.

PROFESSIONAL ORGANIZATION STATEMENTS SUPPORTING TRANSGENDER PEOPLE IN HEALTH CARE:

American Medical Association [AMA]

Resolution: Removing Financial Barriers to Care for Transgender Patients

> "An established body of medical research demonstrates the effectiveness and medical necessity of mental health care, hormone therapy and sex reassignment surgery as forms of therapeutic treatment for many people diagnosed with GID [gender identity disorder] ... Therefore, be it RESOLVED, that the AMA supports public and private health insurance coverage for treatment of gender identity disorder."

American Psychological Association [APA]

Policy on Transgender, Gender Identity & Gender Expression Non-Discrimination

> As stated in the Policy on Transgender, Gender Identity & Gender Expression Non-Discrimination, the APA "opposes all public and private discrimination on the basis of actual or perceived gender identity and expression and urges the repeal of discriminatory laws and policies" and "calls upon psychologists in their professional roles to provide appropriate, nondiscriminatory treatment to transgender and gender variant individuals and encourages psychologists to take a leadership role in working against discrimination towards transgender and gender variant individuals[.]"

> The "APA recognizes the efficacy, benefit and medical necessity of gender transition treatments for appropriately evaluated individuals and calls upon public and private insurers to cover these medically necessary treatments."

American Academy of Family Physicians [AAFP]

Resolution: Transgender Care

In 2007, an AAFP Commission declared that the association has a policy opposing any form of patient discrimination and stated its opposition to the exclusion of transgender health care: "RESOLVED, That the American Academy of Family Physicians endorse payment by third party payors to provide transsexual care benefits for transgender patients."

National Association of Social Workers [NASW]

Committee on Lesbian, Gay, Bisexual, and Transgender Issues, NASW, Position Statement, Transgender and Gender Identity Issues

"NASW supports the rights of all individuals to receive health insurance and other health coverage without discrimination on the basis of gender identity, and specifically without exclusion of services related to transgender or transsexual transition . . . in order to receive medical and mental health services through their primary care physician and the appropriate referrals to medical specialists, which may include hormone replacement therapy, surgical interventions, prosthetic devices, and other medical procedures."

World Professional Association for Transgender Health [WPATH]

Clarification on Medical Necessity of Treatment, Sex Reassignment, and Insurance Coverage in the U.S.A.

WPATH found that decades of experience with the Standards of Care show gender transitions and related care to be accepted, good medical practice and effective treatment. In a 2008 clarification, WPATH stated:

"Sex reassignment, properly indicated and performed as provided by the Standards of Care, has proven to be beneficial and effective in the treatment of individuals with transsexualism, gender identity disorder, and/or gender dysphoria. Sex reassignment plays an undisputed role in contributing toward favorable outcomes, and comprises Real Life Experience, legal name and sex change on identity documents, as well as medically necessary hormone treatment, counseling, psychotherapy, and other medical procedures . . .

The medical procedures attendant to sex reassignment are not 'cosmetic' or 'elective' or for the mere convenience of the patient. These reconstructive procedures are not optional in any meaningful sense, but are understood to be medically necessary for the treatment of the diagnosed condition."

National Commission on Correctional Health Care

Position Statement: Transgender Health Care in Correctional Settings

"The health risks of overlooking the particular needs of transgender inmates are so severe that acknowledgment of the problem and policies that assure appropriate and responsible provision of health care are needed . . .

Because prisons, jails, and juvenile justice facilities have a responsibility to ensure the physical and mental health and well-being of transgender people in their custody, correctional health staff should manage these inmates in a manner that respects the biomedical and psychological aspects of a gender identity disorder (GID) diagnosis."

American Public Health Association [APHA]

The Need for Acknowledging Transgendered Individuals within Research and Clinical Practice

The APHA issued a policy statement concluding that "trans-gendered individuals are not receiving adequate health care, information, or inclusion within research studies because of discrimination by and/or lack of training of health care providers and researchers; therefore . . ."

The APHA thus "Urges researchers and health care workers to be sensitive to the lives of transgendered individuals and treat them with dignity and respect, and not to force them to fit within rigid gender norms. This includes referring to them as the gender with which they identify;

Urges researchers, health care workers, the National Institutes of Health, and the Centers for Disease Control and Prevention to be aware of the distinct health care needs of transgendered individuals; and

Urges the National Institutes of Health and the Centers for Disease Control and Prevention to make available resources, including funding for research, that will enable a better understanding of the health risks of transgendered individuals, especially the barriers they experience within health care settings. . . ."

American College of Obstetricians and Gynecologists

The American College of Obstetricians and Gynecologists, Committee Opinion No. 512: Health Care for Transgender Individuals,

"Transgender individuals face harassment, discrimination, and rejection within our society. Lack of awareness, knowledge, and sensitivity in health care communities eventually leads to inadequate access to, underutilization of, and disparities within the health care system for this population. Although the care for these patients is often managed by a specialty team, obstetrician-gynecologists should be prepared to assist or refer transgender individuals with routine treatment and screening as well as hormonal and surgical therapies. The American College of Obstetricians and Gynecologists opposes discrimination on the basis of gender identity and urges public and private health insurance plans to cover the treatment of gender identity disorder."

10

Sex-Reassignment Surgery Is Unnecessary Mutilation

Julie Bindel

Julie Bindel is a feminist writer who contributes regularly to Standpoint *magazine, the* Guardian, *and other publications. She is the author of* Straight Expectations, *a 2014 book about the lesbian and gay movement.*

Although sex-reassignment surgery has become the standard treatment for individuals with "gender dysphoria" who believe they were born in the wrong bodies, there is no real scientific evidence that such a radical step is effective in eliminating internal conflict and gender confusion. Surgery cannot biologically change a man into a woman or vice versa. The treatment is invasive, brutal, and irreversible, and there is growing concern about the increasing frequency with which children are helped to transition, first with hormone blockers and then later surgeries. Those who speak out and question the transgender movement are harshly attacked for their failure to be politically correct. Sex-change surgery is unnecessary mutilation, and moreover it reinforces gender stereotypes and undermines the feminist struggle for gender equality.

L ast year [2012], I was nominated for the Stonewall Journalist of the Year award. This seemed fair enough since I write prolifically about sexuality and sexual identity. But I guessed that Stonewall would not dare give me the prize, because a powerful lobby affiliated with the lesbian and gay communities had been hounding me for five years. Six weeks later I, along with a police escort, walked past a huge demonstration of transsexuals and their supporters, shouting "Bindel the Bigot". Despite campaigning against gender discrimination, rape, child abuse and domestic violence for 30 years, I have been labelled a bigot because of a column I wrote in 2004 that questioned whether a sex change would make someone a woman or simply a man without a penis. Subsequently, I was "no platformed" by the National Union of Students Women's Campaign, a privilege previously afforded to fascist groups such as the BNP [British National Party, a far-right political group in the United Kingdom]. As a leading feminist writer, I now find that a number of organisations are too frightened to ask me to speak at public events for fear of protests by transsexual lobbyists.

Column Became a Flashpoint

The 2004 column was about a Canadian male-to-female transsexual who had taken a rape crisis centre to court over its decision not to invite her to be a counsellor for rape victims. Feminists tend to be critical of traditional gender roles because they benefit men and oppress women. Transsexualism, by its nature, promotes the idea that it is "natural" for boys to play with guns and girls to play with Barbie dolls. The idea that gender roles are biologically determined rather than socially constructed is the antithesis of feminism.

I wrote: "Those who 'transition' seem to become stereotypical in their appearance—f**k-me shoes and birds' nest hair for the boys; beards, muscles and tattoos for the girls. Think about a world inhabited just by transsexuals. It would look like the set of *Grease*."

Gender dysphoria (GD) was invented in the 1950s by reactionary male psychiatrists in an era when men were men and women were doormats. It is a term used to describe someone who feels strongly that they should belong to the opposite sex and that they were born in the wrong body. GD has no proven genetic or physiological basis.

Apart from Thailand, the country with the highest number of sex-change operations is Iran where, homosexuality is illegal and punishable by death.

A review for the *Guardian* in 2005 of more than 100 international medical studies of post-operative transsexuals by the University of Birmingham's Aggressive Research Intelligence Facility found no robust scientific evidence that gender reassignment surgery was clinically effective. It warned that the results of many gender reassignment studies were unsound because researchers lost track of more than half of the participants.

Surgery's Growing Popularity

The past decade has seen an increase in the number of people diagnosed as transsexual. There are now 1,500–1,600 new referrals a year to one of the handful of gender identity clinics in Britain. About 1,200 receive treatment on the NHS [National Health Service] with the rest going private, Thailand being the main country of choice. The largest clinic, at Charing Cross Hospital in London, saw 780 new referrals last year. The NHS carried out some 150 operations in the last year (up from about 100 in 2005–2006). Apart from Thailand, the country with the highest number of sex-change operations is Iran where, homosexuality is illegal and punishable by death. When sex-change surgery is performed on gay men, they become, in the eyes of the gender defenders, heterosexual women. Transsexual surgery becomes modern-day aversion therapy for gays and lesbians.

In the West, however, supporting the diagnosis and availability of surgical intervention is seen as a view right-thinking liberals should adopt. But no oppressed group ever insisted its emotional distress was the sole basis for the establishment of a right. Indeed, transsexuals, along with those seeking IVF [in-vitro fertilization] and cosmetic surgery, are using the NHS for the pursuit of happiness not health.

Treatment is brutal and the results far from perfect. Male-to-female surgery involves removal of the penis and scrotum and the construction of a "vagina" using the skin from the phallus, breast implants inserted and the trachea shaved. Painful laser treatment to remove hair in the beard area and elsewhere and cosmetic surgery to "feminise" the face is increasingly common.

For female-to-male surgery, breasts, womb and ovaries are removed. Testosterone injections, usually prescribed shortly after the initial diagnosis, result in the growth of facial hair and deepening of the voice.

New Laws Are Harmful to Women and Children

Recent legislation (the Gender Recognition Act, which allows people to change sex and be issued with a new birth certificate) will have a profoundly negative effect on the human rights of women and children. Since 2004, it has been possible for those diagnosed with GD to be assigned the sex of their choice, providing that the person has lived as the opposite sex for two years, has no plans to change back again and can provide evidence of the above.

It is not necessary to have undergone hormone treatment or surgery. In other words, a pre-operative man could apply for a job in a women-only rape counselling service and, if refused on grounds of his sex, could take the employer to court on the grounds that "he" is legally a "she".

A definition of transsexualism used by a number of trans-sexual rights organisations reads:

Students who are gender non-conforming are those whose gender expression (or outward appearance) does not follow traditional gender roles: "feminine boys," "masculine girls" and students who are androgynous, for example. It can also include students who look the way boys and girls are expected to look but participate in activities that are gender nonconforming, like a boy who does ballet. The term "transgender youth" can be used as an umbrella term for all students whose gender identity is different from the sex they were assigned at birth and/or whose gender expression is non-stereotypical.

According to this definition, a girl who plays football is trans-sexual.

Post-Surgery Regrets

A number of transsexuals are beginning to admit that opting for surgery ruined their lives. "I was a messed-up young gay man," says Claudia McClean, a male-to-female transsexual who opted for surgery 20 years ago. "If I had been offered an alternative to a sex change, I would have jumped at the chance." A number of transsexuals I have spoken to tell me how easy it is to be referred for surgery if they trot out a cliche such as, "I felt trapped in the wrong body."

Transsexualism is becoming so normalised that increasing numbers of children are being referred to clinics by their parents. Recently, an 18-month-old baby in Denmark was diagnosed as suffering from GD [gender dysphoria]. Last summer, a primary school headteacher held an assembly to explain that a nine-year-old boy would return as a girl.

Ten years ago, there were an average of six child and adolescent referrals per year in Britain, but in 2008 numbers had increased six-fold. Although the minimum age for sex-change surgery is 18, puberty-blocking hormones can be prescribed to those as young as 16, and transsexual rights lobbyists want that age to be reduced to 13.

James Bellringer is a surgeon at Charing Cross Hospital, which has the largest gender identity clinic in the UK [United Kingdom]. He believes that children should be allowed to self-diagnose as GD. "It is not the doctors saying, 'You are a transsexual, let's get you on hormones,' it is the children saying, 'I don't like my breasts, I feel like a girl.'"

Medical Controversies

There is, however, a dispute within the medical profession about whether puberty-blockers should be prescribed. Some doctors say that children need to experience puberty to know whether they are misplaced in their bodies. I would describe preventing puberty as a modern form of child abuse. Two-thirds of those claiming to be, or diagnosed as, transsexual during childhood become lesbian or gay in later life. "I would be happy living now as a gay man, comfortable in the body I was born with," says McClean. "The prejudice against me for being an effeminate boy who fancied other boys was too much to bear. Changing sex meant I could be normal."

I heard from post-operative trans-sexuals who had been railroaded into surgery and now regretted it.

Medical science cannot turn a biological male into a biological female—it can only alter the appearance of body parts. A trans-sexual "woman" will always be a biological male. A male-to-female transsexual serving a prison sentence for manslaughter and rape won the right to be relocated to a women's jail. Her lawyers argued that her rights were being violated by being unable to live in her role as a woman in a men's jail. Large numbers of female prisoners have experienced childhood abuse and rape and will fail to appreciate the reasons behind a biological man living among them, particularly one who still has the penis with which he raped a woman. (Some transsexuals choose to retain their genitals.)

Critics Face Harsh Backlash

There is a handful of radicals in the world today who have dared to challenge the diagnosis of transsexualism. Those who do are called "transphobic" and treated with staggering vitriol. There is a form of cultural relativism at play here. Defenders of female genital mutilation or forced marriage often use the argument that such practices can be justified within certain communities (i.e. non-Western cultures), despite the fact that they serve to dehumanise women, because it is the "truth" of that particular community. After I had been shortlisted for the Stonewall award, scores of blogs and message boards filled with a call to arms against me.

On one, "Genocide and Julie Bindel", a poster wrote, "What would Stonewall's reaction have been had a BME [black and minority ethnic] group nominated [Iranian leader] Ayatollah Khomeini as Politician of the Year? She is an active oppressor of trans people. I hope she dies an agonising and premature death of cancer in the very near future. It would make the world a better place."

I had some support, some from those who had also experienced a transsexual-led witchhunt. I heard from postoperative trans-sexuals who had been railroaded into surgery and now regretted it. "Do not publish my name," said one, "but if anyone questions the validity of sex-change treatment you are sent to Coventry by the 'community' elders."

A police officer who, during the course of his duty, was unfairly accused by transsexuals of "transphobia" was driven to a breakdown by their vicious campaign. An eminent medical ethicist who had dared to defend a fellow professional who had questioned the diagnosis of GD from a scientific point of view almost lost his career and reputation. And several women from feminist organisations have been bullied and vilified for challenging the "right" of male-to-female transsexuals to work in women-only organisations.

The Need to Question

Dr Caillean McMahon, a US-based forensic psychiatrist, defines herself not as a transsexual but as a "woman of operative history. The trans community has an unforgiving global sort of condemnation towards critical outsiders. I have to be suspicious that the insistence of many of those demanding to enter it is not for the purpose of celebrating the spirit and nature of women, but to seek an enforced validation, extracted by force in a legal or political manner." With the normalisation of transsexual surgery comes an acceptance of other forms of surgery to correct a mental disorder. In 2000, Russell Reid, a psychiatrist who has diagnosed hundreds of people with GD, was involved in controversy over the condition known as Body Dysmorphic Disorder (BDD), where sufferers can experience a desperate urge to rid themselves of a limb. Reid referred two BDD patients to a surgeon for leg amputations. "When I first heard of people wanting amputations, it seemed bizarre in the extreme," he said in a TV documentary. "But then I thought, 'I see transsexuals and they want healthy parts of their body removed in order to adjust to their idealised body image,' and so I think that was the connection for me. I saw that people wanted to have their limbs off with equally as much degree of obsession and need."

In a world where equality between men and women was reality, transsexualism would not exist. The diagnosis of GD needs to be questioned and challenged. We live in a society that, on the whole, respects the human rights of others. Accepting a situation where the surgeon's knife and lifelong hormonal treatment are replacing the acceptance of difference is a scandal. Sex-change surgery is unnecessary mutilation. Using human rights laws to normalise trans-sexualism has resulted in a backward step in the feminist campaign for gender equality. Perhaps we should give up and become men.

11

Transgender Kids: Painful Quest to Be Who They Are

Madison Park

Madison Park is a news producer at CNN International.

Sometimes children know when they are very young that their internal sense of gender identity does not match the body they have. Although many supposed trans children lose their desire to be the other gender as they get older, it is difficult to know whether a child's gender dysphoria is serious enough that it will be permanent. A child's persistent identification with the opposite gender can be especially troubling for parents, who often face severe criticism if they support gender nonconformity or pursue puberty-blocking hormone treatments for their child. There is no good scientific data on transgender children, but experts say that not addressing a child's gender dysphoria could have more damaging consequences in the long run than doing so.

One of the first things Thomas Lobel told his parents was that they were wrong.

The 3-year-old had learned sign language because he had apraxia, a speech impediment that hindered his ability to talk. The toddler pointed to himself and signed, "I am a girl."

"Oh look, he's confused," his parents said. Maybe he mixed up the signs for boy and girl. So they signed back. "No, no. Thomas is a boy."

But the toddler shook his head. "I am a girl," he signed back emphatically.

Regardless of the fact he was physically male, Thomas has always maintained that he is a girl. When teased at school about being quiet and liking dolls, Thomas would repeat his simple response, "I am a girl."

Thomas, now 11, goes by the name of Tammy, wears dresses to school and lives as a girl.

Her parents have been accused by family, friends and others of being reckless, causing their youngest child permanent damage by allowing her to live as a girl.

When children insist that their gender doesn't match their body, it can trigger a confusing, painful odyssey for the family. And most of the time, these families face isolating experiences trying to decide what is best for their kids, especially because transgender issues are viewed as mysterious, and loaded with stigma and judgment.

A Sex-Gender Disconnect

Transgender children experience a disconnect between their sex, which is anatomy, and their gender, which includes behaviors, roles and activities. In Thomas' case, he has a male body, but he prefers female things like skirts and dolls, rather than pants and trucks.

There is little consistent advice for parents, because robust data and studies about transgender children are rare.

Gender identity often gets confused with sexual orientation. The difference is "gender identity is who you are and sexual orientation is who you want to have sex with," said Dr. Johanna Olson, professor of clinical pediatrics at University of Southern California, who treats transgender children.

When talking about young kids around age 3, they're probably not interested in sexual orientation, she said. But experts say some children look like they will be transgender in early childhood, and turn out gay, lesbian or bisexual.

There is little consistent advice for parents, because robust data and studies about transgender children are rare. The rates of people who are transgender vary from 1 in 30,000 to 1 in 1,000, depending on various international studies.

Like Tammy, some children as young as 3, show early signs of gender dysphoria or gender identity disorder, mental health experts who work with transgender children estimate. These children are not intersex—they do not have a physical disorder or malformation of their sexual organs. The gender issue exists in the brain, though whether it's psychological or physiological is debated by experts.

One of the most recognizable transgender celebrities is Chaz Bono, who currently competes on "Dancing with the Stars." Born female to entertainers Sonny and Cher, Bono underwent a transition to become a man in his 40s. He wrote in his book *Transition* that even in his childhood, he had been "aware of a part of me that did not fit."

Many transgender kids report feeling discomfort with their gender as early as they can remember.

Mario, a 14-year-old Californian who asked his full name not be used, was born female. He dresses and acts like a boy, because, he said, since he was 2 years old, he never genuinely felt like a girl.

"I feel uncomfortable in female clothes," said Mario. "I feel like why should I wear this when it's not who I am? Why should I be this fake person?"

But when a child starts identifying with the opposite gender, there is no way to determine whether it's temporary or likely to become permanent.

Children Need Support

"It's important to acknowledge the signs of gender dysphoria, especially for children," said Eli Coleman, who chaired a committee to update treatment guidelines for the World Professional Association for Transgender Health, an international medical group meeting this week [September 2011] in Atlanta, Georgia. "By not addressing it, it could be really more damaging for the child than not."

"It's a very difficult area and there are a lot of children who have gender nonconformity. They will simply grow out of that. Many of them later on identify as gay or lesbian, rather than transgender."

The American Psychological Association warns that "It is not helpful to force the child to act in a more gender-conforming way." When they're forced to conform, some children spiral into depression, behavioral problems and even suicidal thoughts.

Thomas Lobel's metamorphosis can be told in pictures.

After his parents, Pauline Moreno and Debra Lobel, adopted Thomas at age 2, they observed that he was aloof. Shy and freckle-faced, he usually sat in a corner reading a book.

Unlike his two older brothers who were boisterous, athletic and masculine, Thomas was unusually quiet. Because of his speech impediment, he had to go to special education. Despite developing better speech skills, he didn't want to engage in conversation or socialize.

"He seemed so depressed and unhappy all the time," Lobel said. "He didn't enjoy playing. He sat there all the time, not interacting with anybody. He seemed really lonely."

In photos, Thomas appears small with a clenched smile and a glazed and distant look in his eyes.

Throughout his childhood, Thomas wanted to read Wonder Woman comics rather than Superman, wear rhinestone-studded hairbands instead of baseball caps and play with dolls rather than action figures. And, his parents said, he kept insisting he was a girl.

A Serious Red Flag

His situation worsened when Thomas told his parents he wanted to cut off his penis. His parents tried to rationalize with him, warning him that he could bleed to death. But his request was a signal to them that this was serious and required professional help.

After seeing therapists and psychiatrists, the mental health specialists confirmed what Thomas had been saying all along. At age 7, he had gender identity disorder.

The diagnosis was hard for Moreno and Lobel to accept.

"The fact that she's transgender gives her a harder road ahead, an absolute harder road," Moreno said.

They have been accused of terrible parenting by friends, family and others, that "we're pushing her to do this. I'm a lesbian. My partner is a lesbian. That suddenly falls into the fold: 'Oh, you want her to be part of the lifestyle you guys live,'" Moreno said.

Transgender kids do not come from lax parenting where adults "roll over" to their kids' whims.

But that couldn't be further from the truth, they said. People don't understand how a hurting child can break a parent's heart.

"No parent wants to be in this situation," said Lisa Kenney, managing director of Gender Spectrum, a conference for families of gender nonconforming children. "Nobody had a child and imagined this was what would happen."

Parents Are "Tortured"

Transgender kids do not come from lax parenting where adults "roll over" to their kids' whims, said Olson, who treats transgender children.

"The parents are tortured by it," she said. "These are not easy decisions. Parents go through a long process going through this."

Moreno and Lobel allowed their child pick his own clothes at age 8. Thomas chose girl's clothing and also picked four bras. Then, Thomas wanted to change his name to Tammy and use a female pronoun. This is called social transitioning and can include new hairstyles, wardrobe. Aside from mental health therapy, this stage involves no medical interventions. Social transitioning is completely reversible, said Olson, a gender identity specialist.

Every step of the way, her parents told Tammy, "If at any time you want to go back to your boy's clothes, you can go back to Thomas. It's OK." Tammy has declined every time.

She continues to see therapists.

Tammy's room is painted bright golden yellow, decorated with stuffed animals and cluttered with pink glittery tennis shoes. At home, Tammy dances through the hallway, twirling in her pink flower dress.

"As soon as we let him put on a dress, his personality changed from a very sad kid who sat still, didn't do much of anything to a very happy little girl who was thrilled to be alive," Moreno said.

The Hormone Question

This summer, Tammy began the next phase of transition, taking hormone-blocking drugs. This controversial medical treatment prevents children from experiencing puberty.

Girls who feel more like boys take hormone-suppressing medications so they will not develop breasts and start menstruating. Boys who identify as girls can take blockers to avoid developing broad shoulders, deep voice and facial hair. The drugs put their puberty on pause, so they can figure out whether to transition genders.

The hormone blockers are also reversible, because once a child stops taking the drugs, the natural puberty begins, said Dr. Stephen Rosenthal, pediatric endocrinologist at UC [University of California] San Francisco.

But if the child wants to transition to the other gender, he or she can take testosterone or estrogen hormone treatment to go through the puberty of the opposite gender.

This transgender hormone therapy for children is relatively new in the United States after a gender clinic opened in Boston in 2007. Programs for transgender children exist in cities including Los Angeles, Seattle and San Francisco. The kids are treated by pediatric endocrinologists after long evaluations by mental health professionals.

No statistics exist on the number of transgender children taking such medical treatments.

Just a Phase or Something Permanent?

Medical practitioners have to be careful with children with gender identity issues, said Dr. Kenneth Zucker, head of the Gender Identity Service in the Child, Youth, and Family Program and professor at the University of Toronto. Giving children hormone blockers to kids before the age of 13 is too early, he said.

Zucker conducted a study following 109 boys who had gender identity disorder between the ages of 3 and 12. Researchers followed up at the mean age of 20 and found 12% of these boys continued to want to change genders.

"The vast majority of children lose their desire to be of the other gender later," he said. "So what that means is that one should be very cautious in assuming say that a 6-year-old who has strong desire to be of the other gender will feel that way 10 years later."

All of this leads to unsettling answers for families trying to understand their children. No one knows whether a child's gender dysphoria will continue forever or if it is temporary.

The unsatisfying answer repeated by experts is that only time will tell.

Despite the murky science and social stigma that confound adults, Mario, who has lived as a boy since fourth grade, has a simple answer.

"Don't change for nobody else," he said. "Just be you and be happy."

12

Helping Transgender Children Transition Is Child Abuse

Sheila Jeffreys

Sheila Jeffreys is a sexual politics lecturer at the University of Melbourne in Australia and the author of Gender Hurts: A Feminist Analysis of the Politics of Transgenderism.

The practice of "transgendering" young children—giving them drugs to block puberty and then cross-sex hormones until sex-reassignment surgery can be performed at age eighteen—is an alarming and harmful practice that is on the rise in Western countries. There is little data on the long-term health effects because the practice is so new, but it damages bone health, alters height, and leads to irreversible early sterilization from sex-change surgeries; lifelong use of hormones may increase the risk of cancer. The severity and consequences of transgendering children make it a form of child abuse that should be banned. Because transgenderism is based on stereotyped sex roles for both men and women, it also has negative social consequences and undermines the progress of women.

The practice of transgendering children is on the rise in Australia and internationally and should be understood as an 'emerging' harmful cultural practice. In this practice children are diagnosed by psychiatrists as suffering from 'gender identity disorder in childhood' and placed on puberty delaying drugs until they reach 16 years old, and cross sex hormones from then until they are 18, when it is expected that they will have their sexual organs surgically removed. This practice affects both girls and boys, and does not, therefore, fit neatly into the criteria for the recognition of a harmful cultural practice i.e. 'harmful to the health of women and girls'. However, the practice arises from the same source as practices harmful to women and girls, the imposition of stereotypical notions of gender and should, on that basis, be included.

The damaging health consequences of the practice of transgenderism are considerable. For children the practice makes them sterile.

This practice was carried out on three children in Australia in the last decade. Alex, a 13 year old girl, was transgendered after a Family Court of Australia order in 2004. Brodie, a 12 year old girl, was transgendered after such an order in 2008, and Jamie, a 10 year old boy, in 2011. Other children under the age of 18 have also been transgendered in this period, but these three cases have received most attention because of the young age of those so treated. The practice of transgendering children before puberty is on the rise in western countries as a result of a campaign by adult transgendered persons in organisations such as the Gender Identity Research and Education Society (GIRES) in the UK [United Kingdom]. They argue that this practice obviates the need for expensive and difficult surgeries later, when they expect that the children will become adult transgendered persons and require the removal of sexual characteristics. They consider that it will enable the males, in particular, to more easily pass as women, without the height and bone structure that would otherwise make this difficult.

Discrimination on the Basis of Sex

The transgendering of children should be understood as one of those 'customs and practices' which constitute discrimination, not necessarily 'against women' but certainly on the basis of sex. This is an increasing practice which originates in 'prejudices' which are based on the idea of 'stereotyped roles for men and women'. The diagnostic criteria proposed for gender identity disorder in childhood (to be called 'gender dysphoria') for the new version of the US *Diagnostic and Statistical Manual [of Mental Disorders]*, which mental health professionals rely upon, consist specifically of stereotyped roles for the sexes:

- in boys, a strong preference for cross-dressing or simulating female attire

- in girls, a strong preference for wearing only typical masculine clothing and a strong resistance to the wearing of typical feminine clothing

- a strong preference for cross-gender roles in make-believe or fantasy play

- a strong preference for the toys, games, or activities typical of the other gender

- a strong preference for playmates of the other gender

- in boys, a strong rejection of typically masculine toys, games, and activities and a strong avoidance of rough-and-tumble play

- in girls a strong rejection of typically feminine toys, games, and activities.

These criteria render gendered characteristics essential and attach them securely to particular biological sexes in ways which the women's rights as human rights movement has always challenged.

Jamie's Story

The case of 'Jamie' in the Family Court of Australia provides a useful example of how this works. Jamie was one of twin boys of 10 years and 10 months old. Agreement in the Court to the transgendering of Jamie was straightforward because he was identified as 'a very attractive young girl with long blonde hair', that is he conformed really well with cultural stereotypes of what a girl should look like. Jamie's parents gave the necessary evidence to prove that Jamie had the disorder, saying that he 'first began identifying with the female gender when she (the transcript uses female pronouns) was about 2 ½ to 3 ½ years old. She chose female orientated toys, began to identity with female characters on television or in movies, and told her mother: "Mummy, I don't want a willy, I want a vagina." He also 'sought the friendship of girls.' According to his mother, the 'turning point' was when Jamie wanted to wear a 'ball gown' on an outing to see "Phantom of the Opera." Jamie was taken to see a psychiatrist in October 2007, when he was seven years old, and was diagnosed as having gender identity disorder in December that year.

The Damaging Consequences of Transgenderism

Harmful traditional practices are, in the UN [United Nations] definition, damaging to the health of women and girls. The damaging health consequences of the practice of transgenderism are considerable. For children the practice makes them sterile, because if the children are not permitted to experience puberty their ova and semen do not mature. Forced sterilisation and sterilisation of those too young to give consent has been opposed in an international campaign which includes the aim of ending the sterilisation of girls with intellectual disabilities at the behest of their parents. Arguments against the sterilisation of children should be extended to the sterilisation of children through transgendering them. The transgendering of children damages bone health, it alters height, it leads, in girls to early hysterectomies at 18 years, or whenever the surgery to remove sexual organs is carried out, and menopause if the administration of testosterone is interrupted. The lifelong drugs involved have numerous harmful health consequences, such as the danger of liver cancer.

A handbook for parents and professionals on the transgendering of children speaks of other serious effects of the transgendering of children. It says that birth defects may occur in children born to 'transmen taking testosterone prior to pregnancy'. There is no research on this but there is 'anecdotal evidence' of an increased incidence. They also warn that genital surgery can lead to the absence of sexual feeling, and comments that young people may not understand the importance of this. There is no research to indicate how the treatment of prepubertal children will affect their future health because the practice is new and untested. Indeed the international Endocrine Society in its 2009 guidelines on gender identity disorder which recommend puberty delaying drugs for children, does comment that nothing is known about the long term effects of this treatment on the health of the children involved.

Transgenderism Reinforces Gender Stereotypes

Other aspects of harmful cultural practices are clearly applicable to the transgendering of children. For example, a 1995 UN Factsheet says that harmful cultural practices "reflect values and beliefs held by members of a community for periods often spanning generations" and they are for the "benefit of men." The belief that gender roles are biological is a foundational value of male dominant societies, and benefits men because their gender role entitles them to benefits and privileges including servicing by women, and political power. In the case of the transgendering of children, it is assumed that the biologically determined gender role has somehow mistakenly migrated to a child of the wrong sex. Since the role is seen as correct and the body 'wrong', the incongruity is treated by the chemical and surgical reconstruction of the body. The practice of transgendering children shores up stereotypical gender roles and helps to delay the considerable, and inevitable, changes that result from women's greater equality.

Harmful cultural practices "persist" the Factsheet tells us, "because they are not questioned and take on an aura of morality in the eyes of those practicing them."

The practice of transgendering children reveals that stereotypical gender roles are still widely believed, particularly by the medical profession which diagnoses and treats the children, to be desirable and unavoidable. Those who treat children with body changing drugs believe that this is the morally correct course.

A Harmful Cultural Practice

The transgendering of children is increasingly practised in Western countries, and at younger and younger ages, consonant with the fact that the age of puberty is becoming younger. The age at which the surgery is performed is beginning to be reduced also, though the Endocrine Society's guidelines say it should not be performed before 18 years. In Germany in 2009 a 16 year old boy had his genitals removed to become a 'girl'. The severity and significant consequences of this practice, such as sterilisation, suggest that it should be understood as a most egregious harmful cultural practice. Such an understanding would be useful towards bringing this practice to an end.

13

Schools Should Accommodate Transgender Students

Robin Abcarian

Robin Abcarian is a Los Angeles Times *columnist whose work appears mostly online. Her focus is national politics and culture.*

On January 1, 2014, California enacted a law that requires schools to allow transgender students to play on the sports teams and use the restrooms of the gender they publicly identify with. Although school districts that have had similar rules in place for years have not reported problems, the new state law has generated a great deal of backlash, including an effort to repeal the law by voter initiative. The effort failed to gather enough signatures to qualify for the November 2014 ballot. Legal protection for vulnerable transgender minors will not cause the sky to fall, and now that the battle over same-sex marriage is essentially over, society needs to get used to sharing the world with transgender people.

Transgender activist Eli Erlick, 18, was on the phone from her home in the small Mendocino County town of Willits [California] and I could not resist asking her to respond to something uttered recently on the radio by James Dobson, founder of the conservative Christian group Focus on the Family.

"God made us male and female," said Dobson, expressing distaste for California's groundbreaking new law that requires schools to allow transgender students to use the bathrooms and play on the sports teams of the gender they identify with. "You just don't choose gender."

To my surprise, Erlick, a Pitzer College freshman, did not disagree.

"Yes, you don't choose gender," she said. "Why would someone choose? It's not a choice."

Erlick, who was born a boy, told me that she realized at age 8 that she was a girl. She didn't choose to be a girl, she said. She was a girl.

The next six years were not a blissful time in Erlick's life. Her parents were wigged out, she said, and she was isolated in her rural community. In elementary school, when she used the private teachers' bathroom, kids made fun of her. In middle school, there was no private bathroom.

"I could not use the restroom for six years," Erlick said. "I had to go home to pee. I had to pretend to be sick."

School Success and Opportunity Act

The discomfort of a transgender student is low on the list of concerns for many conservative Christians, who, like Dobson, are appalled by the School Success and Opportunity Act, which was introduced by San Francisco Assemblyman Tom Ammiano and became law on Jan. 1, [2014].

"It seems to me it would be a cruel joke to tell a gender-confused child who is being bullied that the solution to his problems is to go use the girls' bathrooms," said Frank Schubert, who is leading a campaign to repeal the law. "That would result in increased bullying, not less."

I asked Erlick to respond.

"First of all," she said, "We are not confused. We know who we are. Being able to participate with your own gender makes life a lot easier—and this is coming from a kid who was not able to for years. There is so much misinformation out there. It's sad to see anyone believing those lies."

Schubert, a political operative, helped orchestrate Proposition 8, which briefly outlawed gay marriage in California. Supported by the Pacific Justice Institute and other well-known gay marriage opponents, he is running a new group, Privacy for All Students, which gathered more than 600,000 signatures, mostly from evangelical Christian churches. About 505,000 signatures must be valid for the measure to qualify for the November ballot. Results will be known by early February. [The effort failed to get enough signatures to appear on the November 2014 ballot.]

Forcing boys and girls to share a bathroom doesn't decrease bullying, it is bullying.

What you often hear from people horrified by the new law is that forcing "normal" students to share a bathroom with a transgender peer amounts to a kind of "reverse-bullying."

Sharing Bathrooms and Showers

"Forcing boys and girls to share a bathroom doesn't decrease bullying, it is bullying," Pacific Justice Institute member Tim LeFever said on Dobson's radio show in November.

School districts in Los Angeles and San Francisco, which have had transgender-friendly policies for years, have not reported problems.

But Gina Gleason, director of faith and public policy at the Calvary Chapel in Chino Hills, told me she doesn't live in Los Angeles or San Francisco, and she doesn't know about that. Her church has worked hard to gather signatures to overturn the law.

"Our heart goes out to any student that doesn't identify as their natural-born gender," she said, but she's worried about students who do not wish to share restrooms or locker rooms with transgender students.

"I remember being in junior high or high school," Gleason said. "Having someone of the opposite sex coming into the locker room, the shower or the bathroom is an uncomfortable thought. We don't believe that children at that age should be forced into those situations."

A Transgender Student Responds

"A transgender girl is a girl," Erlick said. "We don't live in the '60s anymore. People are not undressing in locker rooms. What trans kid wants to expose themselves to other people? That's ridiculous."

From my perch, the fight for gay rights has essentially been won. Same-sex marriage is legal in 17 states and it's probably just a matter of time before it is legal in all 50. Millions of Rose Parade viewers saw two men tie the knot atop a float on New Year's Day [2014] and the sky did not fall.

So why is anyone worried that extending legal protection to vulnerable transgender minors spells the doom of civilization? Schubert, for example, told me he believes the law is "damaging to society," and attempts "to strip society of all gender norms and all gender differences."

John O'Connor, executive director of the pro-LGBT [lesbian, gay, bisexual, and transgender] rights group Equality California, thinks we are seeing a new battle front in an old war.

"The people who existed for years to attack the LGBT community were really focused on marriage," he said. "I think they recognized that they lost, or are losing, and have identified transgender students as their new punching bag." (The Pacific Justice Institute did nothing to refute that idea when it launched a campaign against a Colorado teenager, claiming her presence in the girls' bathroom at her school constituted "harassment." The school vigorously denied it.)

"Until we've walked a mile in their shoes, no one can know what it's like," said O'Connor. "Like everyone, they're just looking for their place in the world."

Folks are just going to have to accept that sometimes that place is a schoolyard, sometimes it's a bathroom, and sometimes it's a sports team.

14

The Wrong Approach to Transgender Students

Mary Rice Hasson

Mary Rice Hasson is a fellow in the Ethics and Public Policy Center's Catholic studies program in Washington, DC.

Children imagine themselves as all sorts of things, but when their fantasies and wishful thinking go too far, it is up to parents to bring them back to reality. The same is true concerning the recent new guidelines on accommodating transgender students in school. Policies that allow children to use the restrooms and locker rooms of the opposite sex and to be referred to by different pronouns simply reinforce a child's confusion about gender. Teacher training about gender identity discrimination is propaganda that promotes a warped view about the difference between male and female. It is all a "big lie" and the state is doing all children a disservice by not reinforcing the reality of two genders.

"Tommy," my childhood playmate, thought he was Superman.

He wore a cape, fought imaginary bad guys, and insisted on being called Superman. His mom and dad played along—until the day "Superman" decided he could fly and jumped off the garage roof. Fortunately, he only broke his arm, not his neck, and his parents went back to calling him Tommy.

Tommy was limited, you might say, by a very concrete, physical reality: he was a boy, not Superman. No matter how hard he imagined, how strongly he believed, and how soaring his lift-off, he would plummet straight down to the ground. He could not fly.

Initially, his parents indulged his childish, wishful thinking. But Tommy's painful collision with reality jarred them back into their authoritative role as parents. Tommy needed their guidance. He needed them to explain the truth inscribed in his body: the 'real Tommy' wasn't Superman—he was a boy. And God made him for something far better than being "Superman." His happiness, not to mention his safety, depended on accepting and embracing that reality.

Fast forward to Massachusetts, 2013.

Just as Tommy needed his parents to ground him in reality, the children of Massachusetts need the adults in their lives to do the same.

But the Massachusetts Board of Education has done the opposite. It recently established a harmful protocol for Massachusetts' public schools, under the benign title, "Creating a Safe and Supportive School Environment." The document offers "guidance" for elementary and secondary schools as they implement new state laws prohibiting gender identity discrimination.

The New Guidelines for Schools

Specifically, schools must remove all "obstacles" which prevent 'transgender or gender non-conforming students' from enjoying "equal educational opportunities." (Massachusetts law defines a 'transgender' student as one "whose gender identity or gender expression is different from that traditionally associated with the assigned sex at birth.")

Much of the outcry centers on three points:

- Transgender children must be allowed to use restrooms and locker rooms of the opposite sex, if they so choose.

- Transgender children may use any name or pronoun, regardless of its biological mismatch (e.g., a boy who identifies as a transgendered girl may insist on being called "she").

- Schools must "eliminate" gendered dress codes and classroom management strategies that divide children by gender.

The Board's policy manufactures 'solutions' to an imaginary problem. It cites the "reality" that children with gender identity issues are enrolled in Massachusetts' schools, but offers no evidence that any of them actually have been excluded from "educational opportunities," such as chemistry, math, or English classes, because of their gender identity.

The Board of Education embraces the queer gospel that each person is a god unto him or herself, creating a gender identity based on feelings, or one's "internalized sense" of self, regardless of biology.

Indoctrination and Propaganda

But facts don't matter to the Massachusetts propagandists. Their real goal has little to do with educational access and everything to do with indoctrinating teachers and children in radical gender theory.

The Massachusetts policy systematically foists a perverse orthodoxy on every public school teacher and child. It promotes the core belief—the big lie—that there is no such thing as human nature or natural distinctions of male and female. Instead, the Board of Education embraces the queer gospel that each person is a god unto him or herself, creating a gender identity based on feelings, or one's "internalized sense" of self, regardless of biology.

"Male and female He created them?" Not in Massachusetts.

The Board of Education insists that schools proactively "create a culture" that would make gender-nonconforming and transgender kids "feel safe, supported, and fully included." But the new transgender-safe culture is insidious. It must be created even if the school currently *has no* transgender or gender-nonconforming children. Why? Liberals presume that unknown numbers of transgender children are suffering alone and in secret, and that they will only 'come out' if the coast is clear.

So everyone must play the transgender game. The indoctrination ("education and training") will be part of every school's "anti-bullying curriculum, student leadership trainings, and staff professional development."

Worse, the Massachusetts Board of Education clearly expects *all* students and teachers to go along with the big lie:

- Students who object to the intrusion on their privacy (from an opposite sex, 'transgender' child in restrooms or changing facilities) will be told, effectively, 'Too bad. Get over it.'

- Students who refuse to go along with the fiction and refer to the transgender child by his or her gender "assigned at birth" instead of the preferred pronoun, will be subject to "discipline." Teachers must "model" the required speech and attitude.

- Schools will train students and teachers in Orwellian [referring to the novels of George Orwell] doublespeak: gender is "assigned" at birth (as if 'male' and 'female' were arbitrary classifications, as random as being assigned to the blue team or red team in gym class) and transgender students may elect "gender-confirming surgeries" (as if double mastectomies, genital removal, and other gender-mutilating surgeries 'confirmed' anything).

- Children will bear the new burden of discovering their gender identity, but will be taught that their bodies offer nary a clue. They will be taught that the transgender identity, perceived as young as "age four," is "innate" and "largely inflexible." (The Board ignores decades of research to the contrary. Dr. Kenneth Zucker, head of the Gender Identity Service at Toronto's Center for Addiction and Mental Health contends that, "The majority of children followed longitudinally appear to lose the diagnosis of GID [gender identity disorder] [by] late adolescence or young adulthood, and appear to have ... a gender identity that matches their natal sex.")

The "Big Lie" vs. the Truth

In Massachusetts, a transgender-supportive culture means that school officials will insist that normal children squelch instinctive reactions that something is wrong when a dress-wearing boy calls himself a girl. Children will be taught that religious truths about sexuality are bigoted relics of a less-enlightened time. They will learn that their bodily reality is nothing more than an arbitrary "assignment" at birth—there is no "human nature," only personal choices and self-definition along a shifting spectrum of human sexuality. Finally, they will be taught not to judge: Who is to say that one's chosen gender identity is any less normal, natural, or good than another?

Remember my friend Tommy? He needed the truth. He needed to embrace his bodily reality instead of wishing for something different.

The children of Massachusetts need the same. The 'Big Lie' can never substitute for the truth.

15

Transgender People Should Be Banned from Military Service

Jeff Allen

Jeff Allen is senior editor and columnist for BarbWire, a conservative Christian website featuring news, politics, and opinion.

A government commission's recommendation in March 2014, to lift the ban on transgender personnel serving in the US armed forces is ridiculous for several reasons. First, the mental stability of such individuals is highly unstable. Second, allowing transgender individuals to serve would compromise military strength and morale. Third, transgender soldiers could face extreme reactions if they are captured by the enemy and their transgender status is discovered; it could get them or other service members killed. Finally, if allowed to serve, transgender people would press the military to pay for expensive hormone treatments and gender-reassignment surgeries, costing taxpayers millions. The US military should maintain its ban on transgender personnel in the armed forces.

A commission led by a former U.S. surgeon general released a report on Thursday [March 13, 2014] stating that the United States should allow cross-dressing transgenders to serve in the armed forces. The panel came to the ridiculous conclusion that there is no reason for the current ban and called on President Barack Obama to immediately lift it.

No reason? What about mental instability? The last thing we need are emotionally disturbed soldiers serving on the front lines. If cross-dressers are so confused that they can't even figure out their own gender, how can we expect them to function properly under the extreme stress of a combat situation?

According to the Associated Press:

> The five-member panel, convened by a think tank at San Francisco State University, said Department of Defense regulations designed to keep transgender people out of the military are based on outdated beliefs that require thousands of current service members either to leave the service or to forego the medical procedures and other changes that could align their bodies and gender identities.

Translation: They want the taxpayers to pay for their hormone treatments and gender reassignment surgeries—just like the recent decision by [Washington] D.C. Mayor Vincent Gray who imposed the same liberal madness on his constituents. Then again, Democrats have always been very generous with other people's money.

It's actually extremely unfair and damaging to morale to force rational troops to accommodate unstable individuals.

Expensive and Unfair

"We determined not only that there is no compelling medical reason for the ban," said the commission led by Dr. Joycelyn Elders, President Bill Clinton's first term surgeon general, "but also that the ban itself is an expensive, damaging and unfair barrier to health care access for the approximately 15,450 transgender personnel who serve currently in the active, Guard and reserve components." (Remember: This is the same Dr. Elders who was fired by Pres. Clinton for her controversial comments about promoting masturbation, and she also pushed for "safer" bullets. Maybe Dr. Elders is now advocating for safer girlie soldiers.)

Expensive? You bet! The panel also estimated that sex change operations would cost about $30,000 each, but perhaps they're hoping to get a group rate for 15,450 candidates.

That ought to keep quite a few doctors busy for a while.

Unfair? It's actually extremely unfair and damaging to morale to force rational troops to accommodate unstable individuals. I predict that we'll soon be paying for more sensitivity indoctrination classes as well. That's not to mention a whole host of other associated complications.

According to the Associated Press, there are a few voices of reason sounding the alarm:

"But Center for Military Readiness President Elaine Donnelly, whose group opposed the repeal of the ban on openly gay troops, predicted that putting transgender people in barracks, showers and other sex-segregated facilities could cause sexual assaults to increase and infringe on the privacy of non-transgender personnel."

"This is putting an extra burden on men and women in the military that they certainly don't need and they don't deserve," Donnelly said.

Compromising Military Strength

Or what happens when a transgender "female" demands the lower strength and endurance standards that are in place for biological women? Talk about weakening our military preparedness!

And what exactly does the Pentagon think would happen to a transgender service member captured in the field of battle in a Middle Eastern country? One thing is for sure, the Muslims won't take too kindly to them "defiling" their holy ground.

That's the problem with this whole crazy idea; it generates more questions than answers and will ultimately open up a huge can of worms. This commission seems to be equally as delusional as the cross-dressers.

The commission's report says that the ban appears rooted in the psychiatric establishment's long-held consensus that people who identify as transgender suffer from a mental disorder. However, that's nothing that some high-pressure, homofascist intimidation and threats can't overcome—just like when the American Psychiatric Association, absent even a shred of scientific evidence, declassified homosexuality as a mental disorder in 1973. Bullying is being rewarded these days, don't you know? . . .

The panel was commissioned by the Palm Center, a think tank based at San Francisco State University, and funded by a $1.3 million grant from Jennifer Pritzker, a Chicago billionaire and former Army lieutenant colonel who came out as transgender last year. Wow, I didn't realize that the going rate for validation these days cost upwards of a cool million dollars!

Backwards Logic

Retired Brigadier General Thomas Kolditz, a former Army commander and West Point professor on the commission, referred to Bradley Manning (a.k.a. "Chelsea" Manning), the Army private convicted of giving classified documents to WikiLeaks, as clear evidence that the stress associated with hiding one's gender identity contributes to irrational behavior.

If these individuals are cracking under the pressure of merely hiding their identities, then what does this commission think might happen under the stress of being captured by the enemy—don't they realize that cross-dressing transgenders might be required to conceal sensitive military secrets? Will they sell out their country under such pressure? Nevertheless, according to this panel, one unhinged traitor proves that our nation needs to revise a proven, two-centuries-old policy and allow the "inmates [to] run the asylum."

The commission recommended that the president issue an executive order allowing transgender people to serve openly. Uh-oh, there's the President's mighty pen again!

The White House on Thursday [March 13, 2014] deflected all inquiries to the Department of Defense. The administration apparently has their hands quite full right now trying to convince everyone that Obamacare [the Affordable Care Act health care reform program] is a good thing.

"At this time there are no plans to change the department's policy and regulations which do not allow transgender individuals to serve in the U.S. military," said Navy Lt. Cmdr. Nate Christensen, a defense department spokesman. But then again, perhaps President Obama will soon "evolve" on this issue as well, but not until after the 2014 midterm elections in November. Democrat evolution always seems to conveniently coincide with the conclusion of elections.

Is it me or am I the only one longing for the good old days, when Corporal Klinger of [the television show] *M.A.S.H.* dressed in drag in order to get OUT of the military?

Honestly, the battlefield is not the place to play Barbie dress up games. It's likely to get people killed.

16

Transgender People Should Be Allowed to Serve in the Military

Melissa Rayworth

Melissa Rayworth is freelance writer and regular contributor to the Associated Press, Salon, *and the news website TakePart.com.*

A government commission considering the question of whether transgender people should be allowed to serve in the US armed forces concluded in March 2014, that there is no medical reason to ban their service and that continuing to do so creates several kinds of hardships for such individuals, jeopardizing their jobs and military benefits and limiting their access to necessary transgender health-care services. The report says the ban on transgender service members is inconsistent with policies that cover other types of reconstructive surgeries or ongoing hormone treatments. Although the Pentagon maintains there are no current plans to revise the policy, the report is an important step toward equality for trans people in the military, currently estimated to be about 15,450 active duty service members.

Life for the estimated 15,450 transgender Americans serving in the U.S. military is more than a fight to survive a combat deployment or endure the impact of post-traumatic stress. It's a daily struggle to keep their identity tightly under wraps.

Despite the 2011 repeal of the "don't ask, don't tell" [DADT] policy, which ended the official persecution of gays in the military, transgender troops who identify themselves as such to a superior officer can still be kicked out of the service. Even if they've earned a spotless record of brave service, transgender warriors can lose their job and benefits and get cut off from a career and community that may be central to their lives.

They don't even have to "tell" to face that punishment. Technically, a commanding officer need only designate a service member as transgender to trigger disciplinary action that could end with removal from military service, says Aaron Belkin, director of the Palm Center, a research initiative based at San Francisco State University's Department of Political Science.

The Palm Center has just released [in March 2014] a study conducted by a nonpartisan team of respected medical and psychological experts led by former surgeon general Dr. Joycelyn Elders and the now-retired Coast Guard director of health and safety, Admiral Alan Steinman.

> *The ban itself is an expensive, damaging and unfair barrier to health care access for the approximately 15,450 transgender personnel who serve currently in the active, Guard and reserve components.*

Their goal? To determine whether U.S. military policies that ban transgender service members are based on medically sound reasoning.

"No Compelling Medical Rationale" for Ban

The commission found "no compelling medical rationale for banning transgender military service, and that eliminating the ban would advance a number of military interests."

They went even further: "We determined ... that the ban itself is an expensive, damaging and unfair barrier to health care access for the approximately 15,450 transgender personnel who serve currently in the active, Guard and reserve components." (The figure was estimated by [University of California Los Angeles] UCLA's Williams Institute, which extrapolated it from numerous data points, including the percentage of transgender veterans.)

One misconception the report dispels is that some medical procedures or treatments transgender people choose would impede their service. "The prohibition on medically necessary cross-sex hormone treatment is inconsistent with the fact that many non-transgender military personnel rely on prescribed medications, including anabolic steroids, even while deployed in combat zones," the report explains.

In addition, the report calls the regulations that keep transgender service members from obtaining gender-confirming surgery "inconsistent with policy concerning other reconstructive surgeries that service members are allowed to have." In fact, the study finds that some of the elective cosmetic procedures that troops receive actually "risk post-operative complications that can be more serious than those of medically necessary gender-confirming surgeries."

The Ability to Serve Openly

Meanwhile, many people who identify as transgender choose not to have any medical procedures. Gene Silvestri, a transgender veteran who does outreach work on behalf of LGBT [lesbian, gay, bisexual, and transgender] veterans and service members, says many transgender warriors are seeking simply to do their jobs and serve the nation. "People are keeping their business to themselves," he says. "We've always been there. LGBT-plus has always served. . . . It's just a matter of being able to do it openly."

Silvestri served as a female and vividly remembers the stress he felt when a superior officer would mistakenly identify him as male. Like many LGBT rights advocates, he sees the data in this report as a useful tool for lobbying to change the lives of the thousands of transgender service members living under the threat of detection.

In the coming months the Palm Center, the National Center for Transgender Equality, Human Rights Campaign, and other organizations will be pressing the subject with the White House and the Department of Defense [DOD]. "The conversation is just beginning," says Belkin.

Will the [Barack] Obama administration choose to remove the ban? Thus far, there's been little indication: Asked about the report during a press briefing earlier this week [March 2014], White House spokesman Jay Carney referred reporters to the Pentagon.

The Pentagon was more blunt: According to *The Guardian*, defense spokesman Lt. Commander Nate Christensen said there were currently "no plans to change the department's policy and regulations which do not allow transgender individuals to serve in the U.S. military."

The Climate Since "Don't Ask, Don't Tell"

DOD's research shows that service members have little concern about the sexual preferences of those who serve alongside them, suggesting that some may feel the same way regarding gender designation. A 2010 study on the potential impact of a repeal of DADT found "a widespread attitude among a solid majority of servicemembers that [it would] not have a negative impact on their ability to conduct their mission."

History is bearing that out: More than two years after DADT was lifted, a 2013 survey of more than 5,000 military families by the nonprofit Blue Star Families found that "a majority of respondents felt the repeal ... had no impact on a variety of issues." Seventy-five percent of respondents, most of whom were military spouses, said the repeal had "no impact on their service member's ability to do his/her job and 72 percent said it had no impact on their service member's desire to re-enlist."

When DADT was repealed, President Obama called the Department of Defense's acceptance of openly gay troops "a tribute to all the patriots who fought and marched for change." That day, then-Secretary of Defense Leon Panetta said he was "committed to removing all of the barriers that would prevent Americans from serving their country and from rising to the highest level of responsibility that their talents and capabilities warrant."

Transgender service members are still waiting for that commitment to be fulfilled.

17

Insurance and Public Programs Should Not Cover Transgender Health Care

Allen B. West

Allen B. West is a Fox News contributor and a senior fellow at the London Center for Policy Research.

The government has no business forcing private health insurance companies to cover sex-change operations and hormone treatments for people who are confused about their gender. Policyholders should not have to subsidize the expense of such expensive elective treatments, just like taxpayers should not be forced to pay for transition-related health care services through public health insurance programs like Medicaid. If transgender people want to alter their bodies with surgery and hormones, it is their right to do so—but they should pay for it themselves.

There is bizarre and then there is just plain absurd. In another case of government telling the private sector what to do—this time in the area of healthcare—the absurdity knows no bounds.

> As reported by the Associated Press, "Insurance companies in the District of Columbia have been ordered to stop denying coverage to transgender residents seeking gender-reassignment surgery. Mayor Vincent Gray says the new

rules will end health-care discrimination against the transgender population. The district joins five states that guarantee such coverage."

A bulletin issued Thursday [February 27, 2014] by the city's Department of Insurance, Securities and Banking says that gender dysphoria is a recognized medical condition. It says the various forms of treatment for that condition, including sex-change procedures, are covered benefits.

So my immediate question is, will Medicaid [the federal government's health care program for the poor] be used to cover these treatments as well? Are American taxpayers now footing the bill for someone to have a sex-change operation? How does that get equal billing with cancer and diabetes?

This is yet another example of a different type of medical condition: liberal progressive mental disorder. Consider the Massachusetts case where a federal appeals court in Boston upheld a judge's ruling that a transsexual inmate convicted of murder is entitled to a taxpayer-funded sex change operation as treatment for her (he is a dude) severe gender identity disorder.

According to Boston.com, in a ruling that was a first of its kind, a three-judge panel of the US Court of Appeals for the First Circuit said courts must not shy away from enforcing the rights of all people, including prisoners. "And receiving medically necessary treatment is one of those rights, even if that treatment strikes some as odd or unorthodox," the court said.

Taxpayer Funding for a Sex Change?

So now a taxpayer-funded sex change operation is a right?

The ruling came in the case of convicted wife killer Michelle L. Kosilek. Formerly named Robert Kosilek, she (he is a dude) struggled for years with feelings that she was a woman inside a man's body. Kosilek's wife, Cheryl, thought she could cure Kosilek, the court said. But Kosilek strangled her in Mansfield [Massachusetts] in 1990 and dumped her body in a car at a mall in North Attleborough. Mayor [of Washington, DC] Gray says people with gender dysphoria, also known as gender identity disorder, "should not have to pay exorbitant out-of-pocket expenses for medically necessary treatment."

So this is how it works folks, progressive socialists—and the gay special interest lobby—find complicit medical professionals to support their assertions. Since gender dysphoria has been declared a valid medical condition, it has to be treated.

The hormone treatments and elaborate surgical procedures are just another new healthcare insurance cost to be shared by others. This is right up there with the insanity in Texas when some rich kid who killed four people in a drunk driving accident was declared to be suffering from a medical condition called "affluenza." Whiskey-Tango-Foxtrot! [A military euphemism for the expression, "What the f---!"]

I hear beard implants are now popular—could that be due to "duckdynastitis?" [referring to the popularity of the *Duck Dynasty* television show]

Individuals Should Bear Costs

If someone wants to alter the parts that God game him/her it is an elective surgical procedure which the individual should pay for themselves. Should the Medicaid and private insurance companies also pay for the change in wardrobe as someone awaits surgery?

Doggone, these liberal progressives just go along and make stuff up to achieve their demented agenda. In the progressive world, no one is responsible for anything. And everyone's emotions and sentiments can be classified as some condition, which the government (read liberal progressives) must take care of—actually the hardworking American taxpayer must pay for.

If you're a fella and not happy with being a fella, and want to be a girl, that's your individual choice. You want to alter your body? Go right ahead and write a check.

And don't give me all that special interest medical condition rhetoric. My taxpayer dollars should not be used this way. Nor should I have to assume the cost of this in my own private healthcare insurance plan.

Organizations to Contact

The editors have compiled the following list of organizations concerned with the issues debated in this book. The descriptions are derived from materials provided by the organizations. All have publications or information available for interested readers. The list was compiled on the date of publication of the present volume; names, addresses, phone and fax numbers, and e-mail and Internet addresses may change. Be aware that many organizations take several weeks or longer to respond to inquiries, so allow as much time as possible.

American Civil Liberties Union (ACLU)—LGBT Project
125 Broad St., 18th Floor, New York, NY   10004
(212) 549-2500
e-mail: info@aclu.org
website: www.aclu.org/lgbt-rights

Through activism in courts, legislatures, and communities nationwide, the American Civil Liberties Union works to defend the individual rights and liberties that the Constitution and laws of the United States guarantee to everyone. The ACLU website has an extensive collection of reports, briefings, and news updates related to transgender issues, and the organization's LGBT (lesbian, gay, bisexual, and transgender) Project is a special campaign dedicated to sexual orientation and gender identity. Publications available from the ACLU include "Know Your Rights: A Guide for Trans and Gender Nonconforming Students," "Handy Tips for Transgender Travelers," and the FAQ "Transgender People and the Law."

American Psychiatric Association
1000 Wilson Blvd., Suite 1825, Arlington, VA   22209-3901
(703) 907-7300
e-mail: apa@psych.org
website: www.psychiatry.org

The American Psychiatric Association is the world's largest psychiatric organization and the primary professional organization for psychiatrists in the United States. The group's website features a collection of position statements, fact sheets, and reports related to transgender issues. The association is best known for publishing the *Diagnostic and Statistical Manual of Mental Disorders* (DSM), the book used worldwide to diagnose psychiatric disorders. In a historic change, the most recent version of the DSM no longer classifies being transgender as a mental disorder. A fact sheet explaining the new description for "gender dysphoria" can be accessed at the organization's website by searching for the phrase "DSM-5 Fact Sheets."

American Psychological Association

750 First St. NE, Washington, DC   20002-4242
(800) 374-2721
e-mail: www.apa.org/email-this.aspx
website: www.apa.org

The American Psychological Association is the world's largest professional association of psychologists, and the organization's website includes more than fifteen hundred reports, news updates, and fact sheets on transgender issues. Titles of note include "Answers to Your Questions About Transgender People, Gender Identity, and Gender Expression," "Transgender Identity Issues in Psychology," and "Gender Diversity and Transgender Identity in Children."

Family Research Council (FRC)

801 G St. NW, Washington, DC   20001
(202) 393-2100 • fax: (202) 393-2134
website: www.frc.org

Founded in 1983, the Family Research Council is a nonprofit organization that is dedicated to advancing faith, family, and freedom in both public policy and culture from a Christian worldview. FRC opposes the transgender rights movement and rejects gender identity and expression laws. FRC hosts a weekly radio show, *Washington Watch Radio*, and the organization's website features numerous research papers, essays, news updates, and blog posts related to transgender issues. Publications of interest include "Homosexual and Transgender Employment Bill Threatens Religious Liberty," "ENDA," and "Gender Identity Protections (Bathroom Bills)."

Focus on the Family

8605 Explorer Dr., Colorado Springs, CO   80920-1051
(800) 232-6459 • fax: (719) 531-3424
e-mail: http://family.custhelp.com/app/ask
website: www.focusonthefamily.com

Focus on the Family is a conservative Christian organization that promotes traditional family values including heterosexual marriage and the view that transgenderism subverts the Biblical roles of men and women. The organization explains its position in the publications "Transgenderism," "Talking Points on Transgenderism," and "Not in My Shower," all available from the Focus on the Family website.

Heritage Foundation

214 Massachusetts Ave. NE, Washington, DC   20002-4999
(202) 546-4400
e-mail: info@heritage.org
website: www.heritage.org

The Heritage Foundation is a conservative think tank that develops and advocates for public policies that promote the ideals of free enterprise, limited government, individual freedom, traditional values, and a strong national defense. The organization opposes recognition and legal protection for transgender people, and resources available on its website include the articles "Sex Change You Can Believe In" and "ENDA Threatens Fundamental Civil Liberties."

Human Rights Campaign (HRC)

1640 Rhode Island Ave. NW, Washington, DC   20036-3278
(800) 777-4723

e-mail: press@hrc.org
website: www.hrc.org

Founded in 1980, Human Rights Campaign is the country's largest organization devoted to achieving full civil rights for lesbian, gay, bisexual, and transgender Americans. The organization engages in political advocacy and grassroots campaigns with more than one million members and supporters nationwide. HRC has been heavily involved in various legal battles related to transgender equality. A special section of the group's website is devoted to transgender issues and includes news and legislative updates, position statements, FAQs, reports, and other resources related to transgender people. The group's 2014 report, *Gender Expansive Youth*, may be of particular interest.

Lambda Legal

120 Wall St., 19th Floor, New York, NY   10005-3904
(212) 809-8585
e-mail: twarnke@lambdalegal.org
website: www.lambdalegal.org

Founded in 1973, Lambda Legal is the nation's oldest and largest legal organization advocating for full recognition of the civil rights of LGBT (lesbian, gay, bisexual, and transgender) people and those with HIV through litigation, education, and public policy work. The organization's Know Your Rights: Transgender website section provides comprehensive information about laws and policies that protect transgender people at the state and federal level—from transgender parenting, to bathroom rights, to health care, to marriage laws.

National Center for Transgender Equality (NCTE)

1325 Massachusetts Ave., Suite 700, Washington, DC   20005
(202) 903-0112 • fax: (202) 393-2241
e-mail: NCTE@NCTEquality.org
website: www.transequality.org

The National Center for Transgender Equality is a nonprofit social justice organization dedicated to advancing the equality of transgender people through advocacy, collaboration, and empowerment. The NCTE website features an extensive collection of research, reports, and news articles related to transgender issues and also provides links to other trans-friendly agencies and organizations.

TransYouth Family Allies (TYFA)

PO Box 1471, Holland, MI 49422-1471
(888) 462-8932
e-mail: info@imatyfa.org
website: www.imatyfa.org

TransYouth Family Allies is a nonprofit that provides transpositive resources to young people, parents, educators, and healthcare professionals. The organization's website features recommended reading lists and links to research and news about transgender issues. TYFA also facilitates Talk Forum, a support and referral source for family members who are negotiating the journey of raising gender variant and transgender children and youth ages three to eighteen.

World Professional Association
for Transgender Health (WPATH)

1300 S Second St., Suite 180, Minneapolis, MN 55454
e-mail: wpath@wpath.org
website: www.wpath.org

Formerly known as the Harry Benjamin International Gender Dysphoria Association, the World Professional Association for Transgender Health is an international multidisciplinary professional association dedicated to the understanding and treatment of individuals with gender identity disorders. The organization believes that sex-reassignment surgery is a medical necessity for many transgender people, and it promotes evidence-based care, education, research, advocacy, public policy, and respect in transgender health. WPATH holds a biennial symposium and publishes *Standards of Care*, a periodically updated edition of the best practices for transgender health care that it first developed in 1979.

Bibliography

Books

Chaz Bono and
Billie Fitzpatrick
Transition: Becoming Who I Was Always Meant to Be. New York: Plume, 2011.

Kate Bornstein
and S. Bear
Bergman
Gender Outlaws: The Next Generation. Berkeley, CA: Seal Press, 2010.

Michelle Boyce
When Dad Becomes Mom: Exploring Trans Parenting. Aylmer, Ontario, Canada: Diversity Training Live, 2010.

Diane Ehrensaft
Gender Born, Gender Made: Raising Healthy Gender-Nonconforming Children. New York: The Experiment, 2011.

Leslie Feinberg
Transgender Warriors. Boston: Beacon, 1997.

Leslie Feinberg
Trans Liberation: Beyond Pink or Blue. Boston: Beacon, 1999.

Jamison Green
Becoming a Visible Man. Nashville, TN: Vanderbilt University Press, 2004.

Joanne Herman
Transgender Explained for Those Who Are Not. Bloomington, IN: Author House, 2009.

Walt Heyer — *Paper Genders: Pulling the Mask Off the Transgender Phenomenon.* Carlsbad, CA: Make Waves Publishing, 2011.

Sheila Jeffreys — *Gender Hurts: A Feminist Analysis of the Politics of Transgenderism.* London, United Kingdom: Routledge, 2014.

Matt Kailey — *Teeny Weenies: And Other Short Subjects.* Parker, CO: Outskirts, 2012.

Susan Kuklin — *Beyond Magenta: Transgender Teens Speak Out.* Somerville, MA: Candlewick, 2014.

Janet Mock — *Redefining Realness: My Path to Womanhood, Identity, Love and So Much More.* New York: Atria, 2014.

Rachel Pepper — *Transitions of the Heart: Stories of Love, Struggle and Acceptance by Mothers of Transgender and Gender Variant Children.* Berkeley, CA: Cleis Press, 2012.

Susan Stryker — *The Transgender Studies Reader.* London, United Kingdom: Routledge, 2006.

Susan Stryker — *Transgender History.* Berkeley, CA: Seal Press; 2008.

Susan Stryker — *The Transgender Studies Reader II.* London, United Kingdom: Routledge, 2013.

Nicholas M. Teich *Transgender 101: A Simple Guide to a Complex Issue.* New York: Columbia University Press, 2012.

Periodicals and Internet Sources

Keith Ablow   "All Wrong—In California, Girls Can Use Urinals in the Boys' Restroom," Fox News, January 14, 2014. www .foxnews.com.

Cecil Adams   "Are Transsexuals Mentally Ill?," *Straight Dope*, August 17, 2012. www.straightdope.com.

Associated Press   "Youths' Gender Identity Treatment Raises Questions," *San Francisco Chronicle*, February 20, 2012.

Peter Baklinski   "Journey to Manhood: A Former 'Transsexual' Tells His Story," LifeSiteNews, November 3, 2011. www.lifesitenews.com.

Carsten Balzer et al.   "A Comparative Review of the Human-Rights Situation of Gender-Variant/Trans People," Transrespect-Transphobia.org, November 2012.

Matt Barber   "Tranny Time: U.S. Military Becoming Global Joke," WND, March 14, 2014. www.wnd.com.

Genny Beemyn   "A Presence in the Past: A Transgender Historiography," *Journal of Women's History*, Winter 2013.

Jacob Bernstein   "In Their Own Terms: The Growing Transgender Presence in Pop Culture," *New York Times*, March 12, 2014.

Dana Beyer   "The LGBT Community's Deafening Silence on Federal Transgender Employment Protections," *Huffington Post*, September 17, 2013. www .huffingtonpost.com.

Aaron Blake and Julie Tate   "Bradley Manning Comes Out as Transgender: 'I am a Female,'" *Washington Post*, August 22, 2013.

Dave Bohon   "California Becomes First State to Pass Dangerous 'Transgender' Law," *New American*, August 15, 2013.

Crosby Burns, Kate Childs Graham, and Sam Menefee-Libey   "Gay and Transgender Discrimination in the Public Sector—Why It's a Problem for State and Local Governments, Employees, and Taxpayers," Center for American Progress, September 2012. www .americanprogress.org.

Jack Byrne   "Discussion Paper: Transgender Health and Human Rights," United Nations Development Programme, December 2013. www.undp.org.

Jack Byrne   "License to Be Yourself—Laws and Advocacy for Legal Gender Recognition of Trans People," Open Society Foundations, May 2014. www.opensocietyfoundations.org.

Matt Byrne   "Maine's Highest Court: Transgender Student's Rights Were Violated," *Portland Press Herald*, January 30, 2014.

Lou Chibbaro Jr.   "Justice Department Launches Transgender Training Program," *Washington Blade*, March 27, 2014.

Loree Cook-Daniels   "Physical and Mental Health of Transgender Older Adults: An At-Risk and Underserved Population," *Gerontologist*, 2014.

Charles C.W. Cooke   "Too Young to Decide: We Can All Agree That Children Should Not Be Able to Change Their Sex," *National Review*, March 6, 2012.

April Dembosky   "Transgender Activist's Death Opens Political Battle," *California Report*, April 18–20, 2014. www.californiareport.org.

M. Dilworth   "Local Officials Push Effort to Repeal Transgender Student Law," *Antelope Valley Times*, September 24, 2013.

Alice Dreger   "Why Gender Dysphoria Should No Longer Be Considered a Medical Disorder," *Pacific Standard*, October 18, 2013. www.psmag.com.

James P. Ehrhard   "Make Way for Transgender High School," *Wall Street Journal*, March 3, 2013.

Kelly Phillips Erb   "Judge Orders Controversial Taxpayer Funded Transgender Surgery for Prisoner," *Forbes*, September 5, 2012.

Diane Erhensaft   "Gender Born, Gender Made," 2014. http://genderborngendermade.com.

Audrey Faye   "This Media Campaign Is as Awesome as Trans-Exclusionary Medicaid Regulations Are Terrible," *Autostraddle*, January 24, 2014. www.autostraddle.com.

Byrgen Finkelman   "Court Takes Couple's Children Because Father Is Transgender," *Times Union*, November 18, 2013.

Nathaniel Frank   "There's No Medical Reason to Keep Transgender People Out of the Military," *Slate*, March 13, 2013. www.slate.com.

Steve Friess   "For Some, Shadow of Regret Cast over Gender Switch," *USA Today*, February 26, 2009.

Gay, Lesbian, Bisexual and Transgender News Network   "Title IX Protects Transgender Students, Federal Agency Says," *San Diego Gay and Lesbian News*, April 29, 2014. http://sdgln.com.

Chris Geidner   "Transgender Breakthrough—EEOC Ruling That Gender-Identity Discrimination Is Covered by Title VII Is a 'Sea Change' That Opens the Doors to Employment Protection for Transgender Americans," *Metro Weekly*, April 23, 2012. www .metroweekly.com.

Eliza Gray   "Transitions," *New Republic*, June 23, 2011.

Eliza Gray   "Barneys Is Counting on 17 Transgender Models for Its Spring Campaign," *TIME*, January 30, 2014.

Jesse Green   "S/He," *New York Magazine*, May 27, 2012.

Thu-Huong Ha   "How Should We Talk About Transgender Issues?," TED Talks, March 31, 2013. http://ideas.ted.com.

Rebecca Hamilton   "Sex Change Surgery Is the New Prefrontal Lobotomy and a Trendy Form of Child Mutilation," *Public Catholic*, May 10, 2013. www.patheos .com/blogs/publiccatholic.

Dani Heffernan   "Dept. of Health and Human Services Could End Medicare's Ban on Transgender Healthcare Coverage," GLAAD, May 2, 2014. www.glaad.org.

Human Rights Campaign   "Supporting and Caring for Our Gender-Expansive Youth," 2013. www.hrc.org.

Human
Rights Campaign

"The Cost of the Closet and the
Rewards of Inclusion," May 2014.
www.hrc.org.

Sharon Jayson

"What 'Transgender' Means, and
How Society Views It," *USA Today*,
September 5, 2013.

Paul Jenkins

"Prop 5 Creates Unnecessary
Patchwork of Special Rights,"
Anchorage Daily News, April 1, 2012.

Leisl Johnson

"From Disorder to Dysphoria:
Transgender Identity and the
DSM-V," *Dot 429*, May 9, 2013.
http://dot429.com.

Zinnia Jones

"The Worst Assimilation of All: How
Modern-Day Drag Hurts Trans
Women and Achieves Little or
Nothing of Value," FreethoughtBlogs,
April 2014. www.freethoughtblogs
.com/zinniajones.

Sam Killermann

"30+ Examples of Cisgender
Privilege," It's Pronounced
Metrosexual, November 2011.
http://itspronouncedmetrosexual.com.

Lisa Leff

"Transgender Advocates Seek New
Diagnostic Terms," *Wisconsin Gazette*,
July 23, 2012. www.wisconsingazette
.com.

Lisa Leff

"Panel Urges End to US Ban on
Transgender Troops," *Atlanta
Journal-Constitution*, March 13, 2014.
www.myajc.com.

Massachusetts Department of Elementary and Secondary Education	"Guidance for Massachusetts Public Schools Creating a Safe and Supportive School Environment—Nondiscrimination on the Basis of Gender Identity," 2013. www.doe.mass.edu.
Kierna Mayo	"To My Trans Family with Love," *Ebony*, November 26, 2013.
Janet Mock, as told to Kierna Mayo	"I Was Born a Boy," *Marie Claire*, May 18, 2011. www.marieclaire.com.
Parker Marie Molloy	"In Their Own Words: LGBT Advocates on the State of Transgender Issues," *Advocate*, December 26, 2013.
Clara Moskowitz	"High Suicide Risk, Prejudice Plague Transgender People," LiveScience, November 19, 2010. www.livescience.com.
Viviane Namaste	"Against Transgender Rights: Understanding the Imperialism of Contemporary Transgender Politics," Trans Bodies Across the Globe, November 9, 2010. http://transgenderglobe.wordpress.com.
National Public Radio	"Laura Jane Grace, Transgender Punk, On Life in Transition," January 19, 2014. www.npr.org.

Sky Obercam   "From Tommy to Tammy: Sex
                   Change Already in Progress for 11
                   Year Old Boy," *Clutch Magazine*,
                   September 30, 2011. www
                   .clutchmagonline.com.

Allison Palmer   "Making Facebook's 'About Me'
                   About Me: How a More Gender
                   Spectrum-Friendly Facebook Came
                   to Be," *Advocate*, February 18, 2014.

Stephanie Pappas   "Mental Health Problems Plague
                   Transgender Kids," LiveScience,
                   February 20, 2012. www
                   .livescience.com.

Stephanie Pappas   "Transgender People New Targets of
                   Hateful Political Ads," LiveScience,
                   August 22, 2012. www.livescience
                   .com.

Wynne Parry   "Normal or Not? When One's
                   Gender Identity Causes Distress,"
                   LiveScience, June 3, 2013.
                   www.livescience.com.

Trudy Ring   "Marriage Equality Is a Trans Issue,
                   Too," *Advocate*, January 9, 2012.

Ryan Sallans   "Transgender Students Rights and
                   Schools: Where Is Our Compassion?,"
                   Ryansallans.com, August 16, 2013.
                   www.ryansallans.com.

Autumn Sandeen   "The Policies Keeping Trans People
                   from Military Service," *Advocate*,
                   March 17, 2014.

Justin Snow

"Right-Wing Coalition Targeting Protections for Transgender Youth," *Metro Weekly*, December 10, 2013. www.metroweekly.com.

Mike Spies

"The Next 'Don't Ask, Don't Tell,'" Vocativ.com, March 18, 2014.

Kat Stoeffel

"All About the Military's Outdated Transgender Ban," *New York Magazine*, May 15, 2014.

Margaret Talbot

"About a Boy: Transgender Surgery at Sixteen," *New Yorker*, March 18, 2013.

Margaret Talbot

"Chelsea Manning's Prison," *New Yorker*, August 30, 2013.

Brynn Tannehill

"We're Not Astroturf: Why Open Trans Military Service Is a Worthy Fight," *Huffington Post*, September 16, 2013. www.huffingtonpost.com.

Brynn Tannehill

"Drag Culture Hurts the Transgender Community," Bilerico.com, March 20, 2014.

Michael Thomas

"LGBTTTT AGENDA: Debasing Society and Corrupting the Nation," State of the Nation, December 23, 2013. http://stateofthenation2012.com.

Traditional Values Coalition

"ENDA Hurts Kids: The Impact on Classrooms," 2013. http://traditionalvalues.org.

Richard Trotter	"Transgender Discrimination and the Law," *Contemporary Issues in Education Research*, February 2010.
Bob Unruh	"Obama 'Destroying Morality' with Transgender Agenda," WND, April 4, 2014. www.wnd.com.
William Van Meter	"Bold Crossings of the Gender Line," *New York Times*, December 8, 2010.
Tom Vanden Brook	"Transgender Troops Serve in Silence," *USA Today*, July 23, 2013.
Julian Vigo	"Transcending the Norms of Gender—The Left Hand of Darkness," *Counterpunch*, June 7, 2013. www.counterpunch.org.
Alix Wall	"Bride Met Soul Mate—Who Happened to Be a Transgender Man," *San Francisco Chronicle*, January 2, 2014.
Jillian Weiss	"The Complicated Rights of Transgender Prisoners," *Advocate*, October 10 2012.

Index

A

B

C

K

L

M